A TIME FO

*Liturgical Resources for
Creation and the
Environment*

Published by Church House Publishing
Church House
Great Smith Street
London SW1P 3AZ

Copyright © The Archbishops' Council 2006, 2015, 2020
First published 2020

Some of the material in this book is extracted from
Common Worship: Times and Seasons (2006), *Common Worship: Daily Prayer* (2005), *Common Worship: Services and Prayers for the Church of England* (2000) and *New Patterns for Worship* (2002).

ISBN 978 1 78140 185 9

All rights reserved. No part of this publication may be reproduced in any form or by any means, electronic or mechanical, including photocopying, recording, or any information storage or retrieval system, except as stated below, without written permission, which should be sought from copyright@churchofengland.org

Texts for local use: the arrangements which apply to local editions of services cover reproduction on a non-commercial basis both for a single occasion and for repeated use. Details are available in A Brief Guide to Liturgical Copyright which is available from www.churchofengland.org/prayer-and-worship/copyright

Scripture quotations are from the New Revised Standard Version of the Bible, Anglicized Edition, copyright © 1989, 1995 by the Division of Christian Education of the National Council of the Churches of Christ in the USA. Used by permission. All rights reserved.

Printed and bound by CPI Group (UK) Ltd, Croydon, CR0 4YY

Designed and typeset by Hugh Hillyard-Parker, Edinburgh

A
TIME
FOR
CREATION

Liturgical Resources for
Creation and the
Environment

A Time for Creation
Liturgical Resources for Creation and the Environment

CONTENTS

Authorization

The orders for Morning and Evening Prayer, Prayer During the Day, and Night Prayer comply with the provisions of A Service of the Word, which is authorized pursuant to Canon B 2 of the Canons of the Church of England for use until further resolution of the General Synod.

The order for the Eucharist complies with the provisions of The Order for the Celebration of Holy Communion also called The Eucharist and The Lord's Supper, which is authorized pursuant to Canon B 2 of the Canons of the Church of England for use until further resolution of the General Synod.

The remaining material in *A Time for Creation* (including the section 'Seasons and Festivals of the Agricultural Year' drawn from *Common Worship: Times and Seasons*, and other material drawn from elsewhere in *Common Worship* and *New Patterns for Worship*) has been commended by the House of Bishops of the General Synod for use by the minister in exercise of his or her discretion under Canon B 5 of the Canons of the Church of England.

Copyright Information

The Archbishops' Council of the Church of England and the other
copyright owners and administrators of texts from Common Worship
and New Patterns for Worship included here have given permission for
the use of their material in local reproductions on a non-commercial
basis which comply with the conditions for reproductions for local use
set out in the Archbishops' Council's *A Brief Guide to Liturgical
Copyright*. This is available from:
www.churchofengland.org/prayer-and-worship/copyright

A reproduction which meets the conditions stated in that booklet may
be made without an application for copyright permission or payment of
a fee, but the following copyright acknowledgement must be included:

*A Time for Creation: Liturgical Resources for Creation and the
Environment*, material from which is included in this service,
is copyright © The Archbishops' Council 2020.

Permission must be obtained in advance for any reproduction which
does not comply with the conditions set out in *A Brief Guide to
Liturgical Copyright*. Applications for permission should be addressed
to: copyright@churchofengland.org

INTRODUCTION

'And he showed me a little thing, the size of a hazelnut, on the palm of my hand, round like a ball. I looked at it thoughtfully and wondered, 'What is this?' And the answer came, 'It is all that is made.' I marvelled that it continued to exist and did not suddenly disintegrate; it was so small. And again my mind supplied the answer, 'It exists, both now and for ever, because God loves it.' In short, everything owes its existence to the love of God. In this 'little thing' I saw three truths. The first is that God made it; the second is that God loves it; and the third is that God sustains it.'[1]

In one of the most famous passages of *Revelations of Divine Love*, the medieval English writer, Julian of Norwich, distils the heart of Christian belief about the all-encompassing love of God our creator. Her words echo the theme of God's loving sovereignty proclaimed in Scripture: 'The earth is the Lord's and all that is in it, the compass of the world and all who live therein' (Psalm 24.1). They constitute a foundational truth for all Christians. We believe that God has created the world and sustains it in being. We also believe that God has uniquely entrusted the care of creation to human beings (Genesis 1.26–30) and that to God we must render an account of our stewardship. And not simply to God, but to our children and grandchildren, who are increasingly clamouring to know what will be their global inheritance.

As members of the global Anglican Communion, we are aware of those around the world who face losing their homes and livelihoods as a result of the effects of climate change. Across the world, people of different nationalities and faiths, and those who profess no faith at all, are using the language of climate emergency and environmental crisis to express their profound concern about the impact of humankind's wilful indifference to the state of the planet. Pictures of oceans clogged with discarded plastic, the desertification of productive farmland, extreme weather conditions, rising sea levels and the catastrophic decline of biodiversity in some parts of the world have introduced an urgency in public and private discourse.

---

[1] *Julian of Norwich, Revelations of Divine Love, 5.*

For too long humankind has taken the environment for granted. Now that we see it threatened, we are at last waking up to the challenge of caring better for God's earth. 'To strive to safeguard the integrity of creation, and sustain and renew the life of the earth,' is one of the Five Marks of Mission.[2] If it is not embraced wholeheartedly and with determination, the other four marks of mission lack credibility. The care of creation is integral to our evangelism and mission.

Praying with creation

The contemplation of the universe should lead us not only to the adoration of our creator, but also to take better responsibility for our actions and repent of our misuse of natural resources. Sadly, as St Augustine observes, in our self-obsession we often fail to make the connection:

> Is there anyone who, contemplating the works of God by which the entire universe is governed and ordered, is not amazed and overwhelmed by a sense of the miraculous? The power and strength of a single grain of seed is itself an amazing thing, inspiring awe in its contemplation. But humanity, preoccupied with its own petty agenda, has lost the capacity to contemplate the works of God by which it should daily render praise to God as creator.[3]

This volume of liturgical resources endeavours to help us re-forge these connections and enliven our praise of God's gifts to us in creation. It is designed to provide the parishes, schools and chaplaincies of the Church of England with a rich selection of liturgical resources with which to worship and pray, mindful of the fact that, as St Paul teaches, creation

---

[2] The five marks of mission have been developed by the Anglican Consultative Council since 1984. They have been widely adopted as an understanding of contemporary mission and were adopted by the General Synod of the Church of England in 1996. In 2012, the ACC added wording to the fourth mark, to include the need for Christians to challenge violence and work for peace.

- To proclaim the Good News of the Kingdom
- To teach, baptise and nurture new believers
- To respond to human need by loving service
- To seek to transform unjust structures of society, to challenge violence of every kind and to pursue peace and reconciliation
- To strive to safeguard the integrity of creation, and sustain and renew the life of the earth.

[3] Augustine, Commentary on St John's Gospel, 8, 1.

itself 'is groaning in travail' (Romans 8.22). Our prayer needs to attend to the voice of creation itself. The sense of the whole creation praying to God finds expression in the spirituality of many early Christian teachers. Tertullian, for example, in his treatise *On Prayer*, says,

> All creation prays. Cattle and wild beasts pray, and bend their knees. As they come from their barns and caves they invariably look up to heaven and call out, lifting up their spirit in their own fashion. The birds too rise and lift themselves up to heaven: instead of hands, they open out their wings in the form of a cross, and give voice to what seems to be a prayer.[4]

Gregory of Nazianzus, writing in the fourth century, says,

> All creatures praise you,
> both those who speak and those that are dumb.
> All creatures bow down before you,
> both those that can think and those that cannot.
> The longing of the universe,
> the groaning of creation reaches out to you.
> Everything that exists prays to you,
> and every creature that can read your universe
> directs to you a hymn of silence.[5]

The idea of creation reaching out to God in prayer is reflected in the liturgy of the Orthodox Church. For example, the Office Hymn for the Sunday before Lent has this verse:

> O Paradise,
> share in the sorrow of Adam who is brought to poverty,
> and with the sound of your leaves pray to the Creator
> that we may not find your gates closed for ever.
> We are fallen;
> in your compassion, have mercy on us.

Francis of Assisi also had a keen sense of creation voicing its praise to our Creator, and the repeated phrase 'praised be you' in his *Canticle of Creation* suggests that each element of creation finds a voice to praise God: "Praised be you, my Lord, by our sister, mother earth, who sustains

---

[4] *Tertullian, On Prayer, 29.*
[5] *Gregory of Nazianzus, Dogmatic Poems, 29.*

and governs us and produces various fruits and coloured flowers and grasses."[6]

Season of Creation

In some parts of the worldwide Church, the month of September is becoming a focus of prayer and environmental action, often climaxing with a celebration of creation on 4 October, the Feast of St Francis of Assisi, or in England with the annual Harvest Festival. The Feast of the Holy Cross, coming midway through September, also presents an opportunity to reflect on the cosmic significance of the cross and to give some welcome Christological grounding to the season.

These developments originated from a proposal of the Ecumenical Patriarch Dimitrios I in 1989. He suggested that the Churches observe 1 September (for the Orthodox the first day of the ecclesiastical year) as a day 'of the protection of the natural environment' and to offer 'prayers and supplications to the Maker of all, both in thanksgiving for the great gift of creation and in petition for its protection and salvation'. The proposal was endorsed by a meeting of Orthodox primates held in Istanbul in 1992. More recently the Anglican Consultative Council at its meeting in Hong Kong in 2019 called for a day of penitence for our misuse of creation, and in February 2020 the General Synod of the Church of England, responding to a sense of urgency about climate change, set new targets for all parts of the Church to work to become carbon 'net zero' by 2030.

In the Church of England, this new 'Season of Creation' has been adopted by some parishes and schools as part of an ecumenical initiative to raise awareness of the urgent ecological challenges facing our generation. In supporting this initiative, rather than invent a new liturgical season, amend the Calendar or authorize a different set of readings to replace those provided in the Lectionary for any particular Sunday, this volume of resources aims to supplement existing texts with a range of liturgical material. Some of the material is newly commissioned, including an Act of Commitment for the Care of Creation. Other material has been garnered from existing texts scattered through the corpus of *Common Worship* which might otherwise be overlooked, such as prayers relating to the Agricultural Year from *Times and Seasons*.

---

[6] *The Cross and Creation in Christian Liturgy and Art*, p.202 (Christopher Irvine)

In gathering this material into one accessible volume, it is hoped that we will grow not only in praise of our creator, but in self-understanding of our stewardship. Delighting in God and delighting in God's creation brings us fully alive as women and men, as the seventeenth century Anglican divine, Thomas Traherne, writes:

> You never enjoy the world aright till the sea itself floweth in your veins, till you are clothed with the heavens, and crowned with the stars, and perceive yourself to be the sole heir of the whole world, and more than so, because men are in it who are every one sole heirs as well as you. Till you can sing and rejoice and delight in God, as misers do in gold, and kings in sceptres, you never enjoy the world. Till your spirit filleth the whole world, and the stars are your jewels; till you are as familiar with the ways of God in all ages as with your walk and table; till you are intimately acquainted with that shady nothing out of which the world was made; till you love men so as to desire their happiness with a thirst equal to the zeal of your own; till you delight in God for being good to all: you never enjoy the world.[7]

+Robert Exon
March 2020

---

[7] *Thomas Traherne, Centuries of Meditations, I, 28-30.*

SERVICES OF THE WORD

Morning Prayer

Preparation

O Lord, open our lips.
All And our mouth shall proclaim your praise.

My heart tells of your word, 'Seek my face.'
All Your face, Lord, will I seek.

Psalm 27.10

One of the following is said:

1 Bless the Lord all you works of the Lord:
Sing God's praise and exalt him for ever.

2 Bless the Lord you heavens:
Sing God's praise and exalt him for ever.

3 Bless the Lord you angels of the Lord:
bless the Lord all you his hosts;
bless the Lord you waters above the heavens:
Sing God's praise and exalt him for ever.

4 Bless the Lord sun and moon:
bless the Lord you stars of heaven;
bless the Lord all rain and dew:
Sing God's praise and exalt him for ever.

5 Bless the Lord all winds that blow:
bless the Lord you fire and heat;
bless the Lord scorching wind and bitter cold:
Sing God's praise and exalt him for ever.

6 Bless the Lord dews and falling snows:
bless the Lord you nights and days;
bless the Lord light and darkness:
Sing God's praise and exalt him for ever.

7   Bless the Lord frost and cold:
bless the Lord you ice and snow;
bless the Lord lightnings and clouds:
Sing God's praise and exalt him for ever.

8   O let the earth bless the Lord:
bless the Lord you mountains and hills;
bless the Lord all that grows in the ground:
Sing God's praise and exalt him for ever.

9   Bless the Lord you springs:
bless the Lord you seas and rivers;
bless the Lord you whales and all that swim in the waters:
Sing God's praise and exalt him for ever.

10   Bless the Lord all birds of the air:
bless the Lord you beasts and cattle;
bless the Lord all people on earth:
Sing God's praise and exalt him for ever.

11   O people of God bless the Lord:
bless the Lord you priests of the Lord;
bless the Lord you servants of the Lord:
Sing God's praise and exalt him for ever.

12   Bless the Lord all you of upright spirit:
bless the Lord you that are holy and humble in heart.

The Song of the Three 35–65

All **Bless the Father, the Son and the Holy Spirit:
Sing God's praise and exalt him for ever.**

(or)

      Blessed are you, Lord God,
creator of heaven and earth.
Your Word calls all things into being,
and the light of dawn awakens us to life.
May your wisdom guide us this day
that we may cherish and care for your good creation,
and offer to you the sacrifice of our lips,
praising you, Father, Son and Holy Spirit.

All **Blessed be God for ever.**

The night has passed, and the day lies open before us;
let us pray with one heart and mind.

Silence is kept.

As we rejoice in the gift of this new day,
so may the light of your presence, O God,
set our hearts on fire with love for you;
now and for ever.

All **Amen.**

The Word of God

Psalmody

One of the psalms suggested on page 34 or Psalm 148

1   Alleluia.
       Praise the Lord from the heavens; ♦
       praise him in the heights.

2   Praise him, all you his angels; ♦
       praise him, all his host.

3   Praise him, sun and moon; ♦
       praise him, all you stars of light.

4   Praise him, heaven of heavens, ♦
       and you waters above the heavens.

5   Let them praise the name of the Lord, ♦
       for he commanded and they were created.

6   He made them fast for ever and ever; ♦
       he gave them a law which shall not pass away.

7   Praise the Lord from the earth, ♦
       you sea monsters and all deeps;

8   Fire and hail, snow and mist, ♦
       tempestuous wind, fulfilling his word;

9   Mountains and all hills, ♦
       fruit trees and all cedars;

10   Wild beasts and all cattle, ♦
       creeping things and birds on the wing;

11 Kings of the earth and all peoples, ♦
    princes and all rulers of the world;

12 Young men and women,
        old and young together; ♦
    let them praise the name of the Lord.

13 For his name only is exalted, ♦
    his splendour above earth and heaven.

14 He has raised up the horn of his people
        and praise for all his faithful servants, ♦
    the children of Israel, a people who are near him.
    Alleluia.

> *Glorious God,*
> *your whole creation sings your marvellous work;*
> *may heaven's praise so echo in our hearts*
> *that we may be good stewards of the earth;*
> *through Jesus Christ our Lord.*

If the psalm prayer is not used, the psalm ends with

All Glory to the Father and to the Son
    and to the Holy Spirit;
    as it was in the beginning is now
    and shall be for ever. Amen.

Scripture Reading

One of the readings suggested on pages 99–100 or

In the beginning when God created the heavens and the earth, the earth was a formless void and darkness covered the face of the deep, while a wind from God swept over the face of the waters. Then God said, 'Let there be light'; and there was light. And God saw that the light was good; and God separated the light from the darkness. God called the light Day, and the darkness he called Night. And there was evening and there was morning, the first day.

Genesis 1.1–5

The reading may be followed by a time of silence.

A suitable song or chant, or a responsory in this or another form, may follow

The heavens proclaim the glory of God:
and the firmament shows his handiwork.

All **The firmament shows God's handiwork:**
And one day pours out its song to another.

The sun goes forth from the ends of the heavens.

All **and proclaims the glory of God.**

Glory to the Father and to the Son and to the Holy Spirit.

All **The heavens proclaim the glory of God:**
and the firmament shows his handiwork.

Psalm 19

Gospel Canticle

The Benedictus (The Song of Zechariah) is said.

Let the fields be joyful and all that is in them:
let all the trees of the wood shout for joy before the Lord.

1   Blessed be the Lord the God of Israel, ♦
    who has come to his people and set them free.

2   He has raised up for us a mighty Saviour, ♦
    born of the house of his servant David.

3   Through his holy prophets God promised of old ♦
    to save us from our enemies,
        from the hands of all that hate us,

4   To show mercy to our ancestors, ♦
    and to remember his holy covenant.

5   This was the oath God swore to our father Abraham: ♦
    to set us free from the hands of our enemies,

6   Free to worship him without fear, ♦
    holy and righteous in his sight
        all the days of our life.

7   And you, child, shall be called the prophet of the Most High, ♦
    for you will go before the Lord to prepare his way,

8   To give his people knowledge of salvation ♦
by the forgiveness of all their sins.

9   In the tender compassion of our God ♦
the dawn from on high shall break upon us,

10   To shine on those who dwell in darkness and the shadow
of death, ♦
and to guide our feet into the way of peace.

Luke 1.68–79

**All Glory to the Father and to the Son
and to the Holy Spirit;
as it was in the beginning is now
and shall be for ever. Amen.**

**Let the fields be joyful and all that is in them:
let all the trees of the wood shout for joy before the Lord.**

Prayers

*One of the forms on pages 65–72 or other suitable prayers may be
used.*

This response may be used

    God of life:
All hear our prayer.

The Collect is said

    Lord our God,
    as with all creation
    we offer you the life of this new day,
    give us grace to love and serve you
    to the praise of Jesus Christ our Lord.
All Amen.

The Lord's Prayer is said

> As our Saviour taught us, so we pray

All **Our Father in heaven,**
hallowed be your name,
your kingdom come,
your will be done,
on earth as in heaven.
Give us today our daily bread.
Forgive us our sins
as we forgive those who sin against us.
Lead us not into temptation
but deliver us from evil.
For the kingdom, the power,
and the glory are yours
now and for ever.
Amen.

The Conclusion

> May God who made heaven and earth bless us and keep us.

All **Amen.**

> Let us bless the Lord.

All **Thanks be to God.**

Prayer During the Day

O God, make speed to save us.
All O Lord, make haste to help us.

Send forth your Spirit, O Lord
All and renew the face of the earth.

from Psalm 104

Praise

A hymn, song, canticle, extempore praise or

We praise you, O God,
we acclaim you as the Lord;
all creation worships you,
the Father everlasting.
To you all angels, all the powers of heaven,
the cherubim and seraphim, sing in endless praise:
Holy, holy, holy Lord, God of power and might,
heaven and earth are full of your glory.

from Te Deum Laudamus

The Word of God

Psalmody

One of the psalms on page 34 or Psalm 19

1   The heavens are telling the glory of God ♦
    and the firmament proclaims his handiwork.

2   One day pours out its song to another ♦
    and one night unfolds knowledge to another.

3   They have neither speech nor language ♦
    and their voices are not heard,

4   Yet their sound has gone out into all lands ♦
    and their words to the ends of the world.

5   In them has he set a tabernacle for the sun, ◆
that comes forth as a bridegroom out of his chamber
      and rejoices as a champion to run his course.

6   It goes forth from the end of the heavens
      and runs to the very end again, ◆
and there is nothing hidden from its heat.

7   The law of the Lord is perfect, reviving the soul; ◆
the testimony of the Lord is sure
      and gives wisdom to the simple.

8   The statutes of the Lord are right and rejoice the heart; ◆
the commandment of the Lord is pure
      and gives light to the eyes.

9   The fear of the Lord is clean and endures for ever; ◆
the judgements of the Lord are true
      and righteous altogether.

10   More to be desired are they than gold,
      more than much fine gold, ◆
sweeter also than honey,
      dripping from the honeycomb.

11   By them also is your servant taught ◆
and in keeping them there is great reward.

12   Who can tell how often they offend? ◆
O cleanse me from my secret faults!

13   Keep your servant also from presumptuous sins
      lest they get dominion over me; ◆
so shall I be undefiled,
      and innocent of great offence.

14   Let the words of my mouth and the meditation of my heart
      be acceptable in your sight, ◆
O Lord, my strength and my redeemer.

Christ, the sun of righteousness,
rise in our hearts this day,
enfold us in the brightness of your love
and bear us at the last to heaven's horizon;
for your love's sake.

If the psalm prayer is not used, the psalm ends with

All **Glory to the Father and to the Son**
 and to the Holy Spirit;
 as it was in the beginning is now
 and shall be for ever. Amen.

Short Reading

One of the readings suggested on pages 99–100 or

The Lord God said, 'As long as the earth endures, seedtime and harvest, cold and heat, summer and winter, day and night, shall not cease.' Then God said to Noah and to his sons with him, 'As for me, I am establishing my covenant with you and your descendants after you, and with every living creature that is with you, the birds, the domestic animals, and every animal of the earth with you, as many as came out of the ark.

Genesis 8.22; 9.8–10

Response

Silence, study, song, or words from Scripture (see pages 42–43), such as

You are worthy, our Lord and God,
All **to receive glory and honour and power.**

For you created all things,
All **and by your will they existed and were created.**

Revelation 4.11

Prayers

One of the forms on pages 65–72 or other suitable prayers may be used.

This response may be used

God of life:
All **hear our prayer.**

*One of the Collects on page 98, or the Collect of the Day, or this
Collect is said*

> Eternal Lord,
> our beginning and our end:
> bring us with the whole creation
> to your glory, hidden through past ages
> and made known
> in Jesus Christ our Lord.

All Amen.

The Lord's Prayer is said

> As our Saviour taught us, so we pray

**All Our Father in heaven,
hallowed be your name,
your kingdom come,
your will be done,
on earth as in heaven.
Give us today our daily bread.
Forgive us our sins
as we forgive those who sin against us.
Lead us not into temptation
but deliver us from evil.
For the kingdom, the power,
and the glory are yours
now and for ever.
Amen.**

The Conclusion

> May God who made heaven and earth bless us and keep us.

All Amen.

> Let us bless the Lord.

All Thanks be to God.

Evening Prayer

Preparation

O God, make speed to save us.
All **O Lord, make haste to help us.**

My heart tells of your word, 'Seek my face.'
All **Your face, Lord, will I seek.**

Psalm 27.10

One of the following is said

Blessed are you, Lord God, King of the universe.
All **Your word brings on the dusk of evening.**

Your wisdom creates both night and day.
All **You determine the cycle of time.**

You arrange the succession of seasons
and establish the stars in their heavenly courses.
All **The Lord of hosts is your name.**

Living and eternal God, rule over us always.
All **Blessed be the Lord, whose word makes evening fall.**

or

Blessed are you, Lord of life.
You make light and darkness,
morning and evening, day and night,
and establish the stars in their heavenly courses.
As evening falls and creatures move on the face of the earth
may we take our rest,
and awake refreshed to praise you,
God, Father, Son and Holy Spirit.
All **Blessed be God for ever.**

That this evening may be holy, good and peaceful,
let us pray with one heart and mind.

Silence is kept.

As our evening prayer rises before you, O God,
so may your mercy come down upon us
to cleanse our hearts
and set us free to sing your praise
now and for ever.

All **Amen.**

The Word of God

Psalmody

One of the psalms suggested on page 34 or Psalm 104.1,21–32

1   Bless the Lord, O my soul. ♦
      O Lord my God, how excellent is your greatness!

21   You appointed the moon to mark the seasons, ♦
      and the sun knows the time for its setting.

22   You make darkness that it may be night, ♦
      in which all the beasts of the forest creep forth.

23   The lions roar for their prey ♦
      and seek their food from God.

24   The sun rises and they are gone ♦
      to lay themselves down in their dens.

25   People go forth to their work ♦
      and to their labour until the evening.

26   O Lord, how manifold are your works! ♦
      In wisdom you have made them all;
         the earth is full of your creatures.

27   There is the sea, spread far and wide, ♦
      and there move creatures beyond number, both small and great.

28   There go the ships, and there is that Leviathan ♦
      which you have made to play in the deep.

29   All of these look to you ♦
      to give them their food in due season.

30   When you give it them, they gather it; ♦
      you open your hand and they are filled with good.

31 When you hide your face they are troubled; ♦
    when you take away their breath,
        they die and return again to the dust.

32 When you send forth your spirit, they are created, ♦
    and you renew the face of the earth.

> Creator God,
> send your Holy Spirit to renew this living world,
> that the whole creation,
> in its groaning and striving,
> may know your loving purpose
> and come to reflect your glory;
> in Jesus Christ our Lord. Amen.

If the psalm prayer is not used, the psalm ends with

**All Glory to the Father and to the Son
    and to the Holy Spirit;
    as it was in the beginning is now
    and shall be for ever. Amen**

Scripture Reading

One of the readings suggested on pages 99–100 or

I consider that the sufferings of this present time are not worth
comparing with the glory about to be revealed to us. For the
creation waits with eager longing for the revealing of the
children of God; for the creation was subjected to futility, not of
its own will but by the will of the one who subjected it, in hope
that the creation itself will be set free from its bondage to decay
and will obtain the freedom of the glory of the children of God.
We know that the whole creation has been groaning in labour
pains until now.

Romans 8.18–22

The reading may be followed by a time of silence.

A suitable song or chant, or a responsory in this or another form, may follow

I will sing for ever of your love, O Lord,

All my lips shall proclaim your faithfulness.

The heavens bear witness to your wonders;

All I will sing for ever of your love, O Lord.

The assembly of your saints proclaims your truth;

All my lips shall proclaim your faithfulness.

Righteousness and justice are the foundation of your throne;
steadfast love and faithfulness go before you.

**All I will sing for ever of your love, O Lord,
my lips shall proclaim your faithfulness.**

from Psalm 89

Gospel Canticle

The Magnificat (The Song of Mary) is said

**The day and the night are yours, O God,
and the sun, the moon and the stars reflect your glory.**

1   My soul proclaims the greatness of the Lord,
       my spirit rejoices in God my Saviour; ♦
    he has looked with favour on his lowly servant.

2   From this day all generations will call me blessed; ♦
    the Almighty has done great things for me
       and holy is his name.

3   He has mercy on those who fear him, ♦
    from generation to generation.

4   He has shown strength with his arm ♦
    and has scattered the proud in their conceit,

5   Casting down the mighty from their thrones ♦
    and lifting up the lowly.

6   He has filled the hungry with good things ♦
    and sent the rich away empty.

7   He has come to the aid of his servant Israel, ♦
     to remember his promise of mercy,

8   The promise made to our ancestors, ♦
     to Abraham and his children for ever.

Luke 1.46-55

All **Glory to the Father and to the Son**
     and to the Holy Spirit;
     as it was in the beginning is now
     and shall be for ever. Amen.

     The day and the night are yours, O God,
     and the sun, the moon and the stars reflect your glory.

Prayers

One of the forms on pages 65–72 or other suitable prayers may be used.

This response may be used

     God of life:
All **hear our prayer.**

One of the Collects on page 98 or the Collect of the Day, or this Collect is said

     Eternal Lord,
     our beginning and our end:
     bring us with the whole creation
     to your glory, hidden through past ages
     and made known
     in Jesus Christ our Lord.
All **Amen.**

The Lord's Prayer is said

As our Saviour taught us, so we pray

All **Our Father in heaven,**
hallowed be your name,
your kingdom come,
your will be done,
on earth as in heaven.
Give us today our daily bread.
Forgive us our sins
as we forgive those who sin against us.
Lead us not into temptation
but deliver us from evil.
For the kingdom, the power,
and the glory are yours
now and for ever.
Amen.

The Conclusion

May God who made heaven and earth bless us and keep us.

All **Amen.**

Let us bless the Lord

All **Thanks be to God.**

Night Prayer (Compline)

Preparation

The Lord almighty grant us a quiet night and a perfect end.

All **Amen.**

Our help is in the name of the Lord

All **who made heaven and earth.**

A period of silence for reflection on the past day may follow.

The following or other suitable words of penitence may be used

We confess to you our lack of care
for the world you have given us.
Lord have mercy,

All **Lord have mercy.**

We confess to you our selfishness
in not sharing the earth's bounty fairly.
Christ have mercy,

All **Christ have mercy.**

We confess to you our failure
to protect resources for others,
Lord have mercy,

All **Lord have mercy.**

May God who loved the world so much
that he sent his Son to be our Saviour
forgive us our sins
and make us holy to serve him in the world,
through Jesus Christ our Lord.

All **Amen.**

O God, make speed to save us.

All **O Lord, make haste to help us.**

All **Glory to the Father and to the Son
and to the Holy Spirit;
as it was in the beginning is now
and shall be for ever. Amen. [Alleluia.]**

The following or another suitable hymn may be sung

The spacious firmament on high,
with all the blue ethereal sky,
and spangled heavens, a shining frame,
their great Original proclaim.

The unwearied sun from day to day
does his Creator's power display,
and publishes to every land
the works of an almighty hand.

Soon as the evening shades prevail
the moon takes up the wondrous tale,
and nightly to the listening earth
repeats the story of her birth;

Whilst all the stars that round her burn,
and all the planets in their turn,
confirm the tidings, as they roll,
and spread the truth from pole to pole.

What though in solemn silence all
move round the dark terrestrial ball;
what though nor real voice nor sound
amid their radiant orbs he found;

In reason's ear they all rejoice,
and utter forth a glorious voice;
for ever singing as they shine,
'the hand that made us is divine.'

(May be sung to Te Lucis Ante Terminum, Mode viii)

The Word of God

Psalmody

One or both of the following psalms may be used.

Psalm 65

1   Praise is due to you, O God, in Zion; ♦
     to you that answer prayer shall vows be paid.

2   To you shall all flesh come to confess their sins; ♦
    when our misdeeds prevail against us,
        you will purge them away.

3   Happy are they whom you choose
        and draw to your courts to dwell there. ♦
    We shall be satisfied with the blessings of your house,
        even of your holy temple.

4   With wonders you will answer us in your righteousness,
        O God of our salvation, ♦
    O hope of all the ends of the earth
        and of the farthest seas.

5   In your strength you set fast the mountains ♦
    and are girded about with might.

6   You still the raging of the seas, ♦
    the roaring of their waves
        and the clamour of the peoples.

7   Those who dwell at the ends of the earth
        tremble at your marvels; ♦
    the gates of the morning and evening sing your praise.

8   You visit the earth and water it; ♦
        you make it very plenteous.

9   The river of God is full of water; ♦
    you prepare grain for your people,
        for so you provide for the earth.

10 You drench the furrows and smooth out the ridges; ♦
    you soften the ground with showers and bless its increase.

11 You crown the year with your goodness, ♦
    and your paths overflow with plenty.

12 May the pastures of the wilderness flow with goodness ♦
    and the hills be girded with joy.

13 May the meadows be clothed with flocks of sheep ♦
    and the valleys stand so thick with corn
        that they shall laugh and sing.

or

Psalm 134

1   Come, bless the Lord, all you servants of the Lord, ♦
    you that by night stand in the house of the Lord.

2   Lift up your hands towards the sanctuary ♦
    and bless the Lord.

3   The Lord who made heaven and earth ♦
    give you blessing out of Zion.

At the end of the psalmody, the following is said or sung

**All   Glory to the Father and to the Son
     and to the Holy Spirit;
     as it was in the beginning is now
     and shall be for ever. Amen.**

Scripture Reading

One of the following short lessons or another suitable passage is read.

God saw everything that he had made, and indeed, it was
very good.

Genesis 1.31

O Lord, how manifold are your works! In wisdom you have
made them all; the earth is full of your creatures.

Psalm 104.26

In Christ all things in heaven and on earth were created,
things visible and invisible ... all things have been created
through him and for him.

Colossians 1.16

You are worthy, our Lord and God, to receive glory and honour
and power, for you created all things, and by your will they
existed and were created.

Revelation 4.11

The following responsory may be said

Into your hands, O Lord, I commend my spirit.
All Into your hands, O Lord, I commend my spirit.

For you have redeemed me, Lord God of truth.
All I commend my spirit.

Glory to the Father and to the Son
and to the Holy Spirit.
All Into your hands, O Lord, I commend my spirit.

Keep me, O Lord, as the apple of your eye. [Alleluia.]
All Hide me under the shadow of your wings. [Alleluia.]

The Gospel Canticle

The Nunc dimittis (the Song of Simeon) is said or sung

In you, O Christ, there is a new creation.
The old has passed away, and all things are being made anew.

Now, Lord, you let your servant go in peace: ♦
your word has been fulfilled.

My own eyes have seen the salvation ♦
which you have prepared in the sight of every people;

A light to reveal you to the nations ♦
and the glory of your people Israel.

Luke 2.29–32

All Glory to the Father and to the Son
and to the Holy Spirit;
as it was in the beginning is now
and shall be for ever. Amen.

In you, O Christ, there is a new creation.
The old has passed away, and all things are being made anew.

2 Corinthians 5.17 (adapted)

The Prayers

Intercessions and thanksgivings may be offered here.

Collect

Heavenly Father and Lord of Life,
you have created the heavens and the earth,
the sun and the earth, the moon and the stars.
Grant that as now we take our rest,
we may awake strengthened to serve you
in the care of your good creation,
and with a song of praise on our lips;
through Jesus Christ, our Lord.

All Amen.

The Lord's Prayer may be said.

**All Our Father, who art in heaven,
hallowed be thy name;
thy kingdom come;
thy will be done;
on earth as it is in heaven.
Give us this day our daily bread.
And forgive us our trespasses,
as we forgive those who trespass against us.
And lead us not into temptation;
but deliver us from evil.
For thine is the kingdom,
the power and the glory,
for ever and ever.
Amen.**

In peace we will lie down and sleep;
All **for you alone, Lord, make us dwell in safety.**

Abide with us, Lord Jesus,
All **for the night is at hand and the day is now past.**

As the night watch looks for the morning,
All **so do we look for you, O Christ.**

[Come with the dawning of the day
All **and make yourself known in the breaking of the bread.]**

The Lord bless us and watch over us;
the Lord make his face shine upon us and be gracious to us;
the Lord look kindly on us and give us peace.
All **Amen.**

ALTERNATIVE PSALMS AND CANTICLES IN DAILY PRAYER

Psalms

8	O Lord our governor
19	The heavens are telling the glory of God
24	The earth is the Lord's
33	Rejoice in the Lord, O you righteous
65	Praise is due to you, O God, in Zion
80	Hear, O Shepherd of Israel
90.1–6, 13–end	Lord, you have been our refuge
96	Sing to the Lord a new song
100	O be joyful in the Lord
103	Bless the Lord, O my soul
104.25–37	People go forth to their work
106	Alleluia. Give thanks to the Lord, for he is gracious
107	O give thanks to the Lord, for he is gracious
112	Alleluia. Blessed are those who fear the Lord
126	When the Lord restored the fortunes of Zion
136.1–9, 23–26	Give thanks to the Lord, for he is gracious
146	Alleluia. Praise the Lord, O my soul
147.1–13	Alleluia. How good it is to make music for our God
148	Alleluia. Praise the Lord from the heavens

Canticles

A Song of the Wilderness

All **Lift up your voice with strength,**
 O herald of good tidings.

1 The wilderness and the dry land shall rejoice, ♦
 the desert shall blossom and burst into song.

2 They shall see the glory of the Lord, ♦
 the majesty of our God.

3 Strengthen the weary hands, ♦
 and make firm the feeble knees.

4 Say to the anxious, 'Be strong, fear not,
 your God is coming with judgement, ♦
 coming with judgement to save you.'

5 Then shall the eyes of the blind be opened, ♦
 and the ears of the deaf unstopped;

6 Then shall the lame leap like a hart, ♦
 and the tongue of the dumb sing for joy.

7 For waters shall break forth in the wilderness, ♦
 and streams in the desert;

8 The ransomed of the Lord shall return with singing, ♦
 with everlasting joy upon their heads.

9 Joy and gladness shall be theirs, ♦
 and sorrow and sighing shall flee away.

Isaiah 35.1,2b–4a,4c–6,10

All **Glory to the Father and to the Son**
 and to the Holy Spirit;
 as it was in the beginning is now
 and shall be for ever. Amen.

All **Lift up your voice with strength,**
 O herald of good tidings.

A Song of the New Creation

All **I will make a way in the wilderness,
and rivers in the desert.**

1   'I am the Lord, your Holy One, ♦
     the Creator of Israel, your King.'

2   Thus says the Lord, who makes a way in the sea, ♦
     a path in the mighty waters,

3   'Remember not the former things, ♦
     nor consider the things of old.

4   'Behold, I am doing a new thing; ♦
     now it springs forth, do you not perceive it?

5   'I will make a way in the wilderness
         and rivers in the desert, ♦
     to give drink to my chosen people,

6   'The people whom I formed for myself, ♦
     that they might declare my praise.'

Isaiah 43.15,16,18,19,20c,21

All **Glory to the Father and to the Son
and to the Holy Spirit;
as it was in the beginning is now
and shall be for ever. Amen.**

All **I will make a way in the wilderness,
and rivers in the desert.**

A Song of Creation (Benedicite) (a)

1   Bless the Lord all you works of the Lord:
    Sing God's praise and exalt him for ever.

2   Bless the Lord you heavens:
    Sing God's praise and exalt him for ever.

3   Bless the Lord you angels of the Lord:
    bless the Lord all you his hosts;
    bless the Lord you waters above the heavens:
    Sing God's praise and exalt him for ever.

4   Bless the Lord sun and moon:
    bless the Lord you stars of heaven;
    bless the Lord all rain and dew:
    Sing God's praise and exalt him for ever.

5   Bless the Lord all winds that blow:
    bless the Lord you fire and heat;
    bless the Lord scorching wind and bitter cold:
    Sing God's praise and exalt him for ever.

6   Bless the Lord dews and falling snows:
    bless the Lord you nights and days;
    bless the Lord light and darkness:
    Sing God's praise and exalt him for ever.

7   Bless the Lord frost and cold:
    bless the Lord you ice and snow;
    bless the Lord lightnings and clouds:
    Sing God's praise and exalt him for ever.

8   O let the earth bless the Lord:
    bless the Lord you mountains and hills;
    bless the Lord all that grows in the ground:
    Sing God's praise and exalt him for ever.

9   Bless the Lord you springs:
    bless the Lord you seas and rivers;
    bless the Lord you whales and all that swim in the waters:
    Sing God's praise and exalt him for ever.

10 Bless the Lord all birds of the air:
bless the Lord you beasts and cattle;
bless the Lord all people on earth:
Sing God's praise and exalt him for ever.

11 O people of God bless the Lord:
bless the Lord you priests of the Lord;
bless the Lord you servants of the Lord:
Sing God's praise and exalt him for ever.

12 Bless the Lord all you of upright spirit:
bless the Lord you that are holy and humble in heart.

The Song of the Three 35–65

**All Bless the Father, the Son and the Holy Spirit:
Sing God's praise and exalt him for ever.**

A Song of Creation (Benedicite) (b)

1 Bless the Lord all you works of the Lord: ♦
sing his praise and exalt him for ever.

2 Bless the Lord you heavens: ♦
sing his praise and exalt him for ever.

3 Bless the Lord you angels of the Lord: ♦
sing his praise and exalt him for ever.

4 Bless the Lord all people on earth: ♦
sing his praise and exalt him for ever.

5 O people of God bless the Lord: ♦
sing his praise and exalt him for ever.

6 Bless the Lord you priests of the Lord: ♦
sing his praise and exalt him for ever.

7 Bless the Lord you servants of the Lord: ♦
sing his praise and exalt him for ever.

8 Bless the Lord all you of upright spirit: ♦
bless the Lord you that are holy and humble in heart.

The Song of the Three 35–37, 60–65

**All Bless the Father, the Son and the Holy Spirit: ♦
sing his praise and exalt him for ever.**

A Song of Praise

All **You created all things, O God,**
and are worthy of our praise for ever.

1   You are worthy, our Lord and God, ◆
to receive glory and honour and power.

2   For you have created all things, ◆
and by your will they have their being.

3   You are worthy, O Lamb, for you were slain, ◆
and by your blood you ransomed for God
saints from every tribe and language and nation.

4   You have made them to be a kingdom and priests
serving our God, ◆
and they will reign with you on earth.

Revelation 4.11; 5.9b,10

All **To the One who sits on the throne and to the Lamb** ◆
be blessing and honour and glory and might,
for ever and ever. Amen.

All **You created all things, O God,**
and are worthy of our praise for ever.

A Song of the Holy City

All **I saw the holy city**
coming down out of heaven from God.

1   I saw a new heaven and a new earth, ◆
for the first heaven and the first earth had passed away
and the sea was no more.

2   And I saw the holy city, new Jerusalem,
coming down out of heaven from God, ◆
prepared as a bride adorned for her husband.

3   And I heard a great voice from the throne saying, ◆
'Behold, the dwelling of God is among mortals.

4   'He will dwell with them and they shall be his peoples, ◆
and God himself will be with them.

5   'He will wipe every tear from their eyes, ♦
     and death shall be no more.

6   'Neither shall there be mourning,
          nor crying, nor pain any more, ♦
     for the former things have passed away.'

7   And the One who sat upon the throne said, ♦
     'Behold, I make all things new.'

Revelation 21.1–5a

All **To the One who sits on the throne and to the Lamb ♦
     be blessing and honour and glory and might,
     for ever and ever. Amen.**

All **I saw the holy city
     coming down out of heaven from God.**

A Song of Francis of Assisi

1   Most High, all powerful, good Lord, ♦
     to you be praise, glory, honour and all blessing.

2   Only to you, Most High, do they belong ♦
     and no one is worthy to call upon your name.

3   May you be praised, my Lord, with all your creatures,
          especially brother sun, ♦
     through whom you lighten the day for us.

4   He is beautiful and radiant with great splendour; ♦
     he signifies you, O Most High.

5   Be praised, my Lord, for sister moon and the stars: ♦
     clear and precious and lovely, they are formed in heaven.

6   Be praised, my Lord, for brother wind; ♦
     for air and clouds, clear skies and all weathers,
          by which you give sustenance to your creatures.

7   Be praised, my Lord, for sister water, ♦
     who is very useful and humble and precious and pure.

8   Be praised, my Lord, for brother fire,
         by whom the night is illumined for us: ♦
     he is beautiful and cheerful, full of power and strength.

9   Be praised, my Lord, for our sister, mother earth,
         who sustains and governs us ♦
     and produces diverse fruits
         and coloured flowers and grass.

10   Be praised, my Lord, by all those who forgive for love of you ♦
     and who bear weakness and tribulation.

11   Blessed are those who bear them in peace: ♦
     for you, Most High, they will be crowned.

12   Be praised, my Lord, for our sister, the death of the body,
         from which no one living is able to flee; ♦
     woe to those who are dying in mortal sin.

13   Blessed are those who are found doing your most holy will, ♦
     for the second death will do them no harm.

14   Praise and bless my Lord and give him thanks ♦
     and serve him with great humility.

SHORT PASSAGES OF SCRIPTURE

1   God saw everything that he had made,
     and indeed, it was very good.   *Genesis 1.31*

2   Let the peoples praise you, O God;
     let all the peoples praise you.
     The earth has yielded its increase;
     God, our God, has blessed us.   *Psalm 67.5,6*

3   The Lord will indeed give all that is good,
     and our land will yield its increase.   *Psalm 85.12*

4   O Lord, how manifold are your works!
     In wisdom you have made them all;
     the earth is full of your creatures.   *Psalm 104.26*

5   Those who are generous are blessed,
     for they share their bread with the poor.   *Proverbs 22.9*

6   For as the rain and the snow come down from heaven,
     and do not return there until they have watered the earth,
     making it bring forth and sprout,
     giving seed to the sower and bread to the eater,
     so shall my word be that goes out from my mouth;
     it shall not return to me empty,
     but it shall accomplish that which I purpose,
     and succeed in the thing for which I sent it.
                             Isaiah 55.10–11

7   Sow for yourselves righteousness;
     reap steadfast love;
     break up your fallow ground;
     for it is time to seek the Lord,
     that he may come and rain righteousness upon you. *Hosea 10.12*

8   He who supplies seed to the sower and bread for food
     will supply and multiply your seed for sowing
     and increase the harvest of your righteousness.
                           2 Corinthians 9.10

9   In Christ all things in heaven and on earth were created,
     things visible and invisible ... all things have been created
     through him and for him.

Colossians 1.16

10   You are worthy, our Lord and God,
     to receive glory and honour and power,
     for you created all things,
     and by your will they existed and were created.   *Revelation 4.11*

PRAYERS FOR THE ENVIRONMENT

A lament for a time of global environmental and climate crisis

The following lament has been composed from various scriptural texts to voice our grief in the face of this global environmental crisis. 'Take words with you and return to the Lord; say to him, "Take away all guilt; accept that which is good, and we will offer the fruit of our lips" (Hosea 14.2). As the Psalms give witness, in worship we come before the Lord not only with words of praise, but also of lament to express our grief and sorrow.

In shaping its use in worship, it may be appropriate for the leader to keep a space for silence either between the verses, for reflection, or before the lament is recited. Such a period of silence may conclude with the words, 'Lord, hear our cry'.

Refrain

All The land cries out to you, O Lord.

1 The land mourns: and all who dwell on it languish.

2 The beasts of the field, the birds of the air: and even the fish of the sea are perishing. *(Hosea 4.3)*

3 For the earth is scorched with fire: the air polluted, and the waters choked with waste.

4 The ice melts and the seas rage: the waters surge and floods devastate the land.

5 The water springs are silent, and the steams run dry: the green places are a dry land where there is no water. *(Psalm 63.2b)*

6 The fertile ground is exhausted: the land has become a parched and windswept wasteland.

7 The holy cities have become a wilderness: Zion has become a desolation. *(Isaiah 64.10)*

8 So turn us again, O Lord: and come to our help. *(Psalm 80.4a,3b)*

9   Drop down, O heavens, from above: and let righteousness rain down upon the poor. *(Isaiah 45.8)*

10   Let the earth open: and let wholeness and healing spring forth. *(Isaiah 45.8b)*

11   Then the wilderness and the dry land shall be glad:
the desert shall rejoice and blossom. *(Isaiah 35.1)*

12   The mountains and hills shall break forth into singing:
and the trees of the forest shall clap their hands. *(Isaiah 55.12b)*

All **Glory to the Father and to the Son
and to the Holy Spirit;
as it was in the beginning is now
and shall be for ever. Amen.**

All **The land cries out to you, O Lord.**

A prayer for the farming community in a time of crisis

God of life and hope,
you sent us from the garden of Eden
to till the soil and to grow our food by the sweat of our brow,
but in your love you never cease to watch over us;
Look upon the land and all who tend it at this time of crisis.
We pray for…

As we stand before you in prayer,
we pray for all who are suffering.
We acknowledge our dependence on your creation for our food,
and ask that your compassion remain with us and with all for
whom we pray;
in the name of Jesus Christ our Lord.

All **Amen.**

Prayers in times of extreme weather

1   O God of heaven and earth,
     whose Son commanded the elements at the sea of Galilee,
     we pray to you now as we witness weather that threatens
     the land,
     the plants and animals we share it with and depend upon
     for our food.
     Send us, we ask you, in this time of need,
        [relief from wind and storm]
        [relief from rain and flood]
        [such moderate rain and showers]
     that the land may recover
     and we with all creation may enjoy the fruits of the earth,
     to our comfort and to your praise,
     through Jesus Christ our Lord.
All **Amen.**

2   God our creator, create in us a new heart,
     a new understanding, a new way of living.
     God our Redeemer, rescue us from the brink of disaster,
     open our eyes to see the dangers that lie ahead.
     God our Sustainer, equip and energize us,
     to hold fast to the changes that we need to make.
All **Amen.**

A prayer for the waters and the seas

     Let the heavens and the earth praise you, O Lord:
All **the seas and all that move in them.**   *Psalm 69.36*

Readings

Isaiah 43.15–19   The Lord makes a way in the sea
Mark 6.45–51   The Lord of nature
John 21.1–8   The risen Lord appears on the shore of the sea
                   of Galilee

Psalm 107.23–32

23 Those who go down to the sea in ships
    and ply their trade in great waters,

24 These have seen the works of the Lord
    and his wonders in the deep.

25 For at his word the stormy wind arose
    and lifted up the waves of the sea.

26 They were carried up to the heavens
        and down again to the deep;
    their soul melted away in their peril.

27 They reeled and staggered like a drunkard
    and were at their wits' end.

28 Then they cried to the Lord in their trouble,
    and he brought them out of their distress.

29 He made the storm be still
    and the waves of the sea were calmed.

30 Then were they glad because they were at rest,
    and he brought them to the haven they desired.

All **Let us give thanks to the Lord for his goodness,
and for the wonders he does for his children.
Let us exalt him in the congregation of the people,
and praise him in the council of elders.**

Eternal Father, strong to save,
whose Spirit hovered over the deep
and filled it with innumerable living things:
may our seas, lakes, and rivers teem with life;
be kept pure and free from pollution.
May all those who move through the waters
wonder at its marvels, be protected from its perils,
and be brought to the haven they desire,
through Jesus Christ our Lord.

All **Amen.**

An act of commitment for the care of creation

'While all creatures stand in expectation, what will be the result
of our liberty?'

(Thomas Traherne)

As the whole of creation looks with eager longing for the redemption
of humankind, let us pledge ourselves anew to serve our Creator
God, the Father who is the maker of all things,
the Son through whom all things are made, and the Holy Spirit,
the giver of life, who renews the face of the earth.

Let us stand to affirm our commitment to care actively for God's
creation.

All   **Lord of life and giver of hope,**
we pledge ourselves to care for creation,
to reduce our waste,
to live sustainably,
and to value the rich diversity of life.
May your wisdom guide us,
that life in all its forms may flourish,
and may be faithful in voicing creation's praise.

May the commitment we have made this day be matched by our
faithful living.

All   **Amen. Amen. Amen.**

EUCHARIST

From earliest times Christians have gathered together to celebrate the Eucharist. Indeed, the Acts of the Apostles suggests that the 'breaking of bread' was the defining practice of the first Christian community. The word eucharist literally means 'thanksgiving', and thanks are made over bread and wine, the fruit of the earth and of the vine. The thanksgiving prayer, here as elsewhere, has a trinitarian shape as we give thanks for the work of the triune God in and through creation, setting it free, and making all things new.

In the order of service provided here, we recognise that the earth is God's gift, and that we ourselves, being made in the image of God, are called to care for this fragile planet earth, to share its resources justly and to protect the variety of life it sustains. And so, in the Prayers of Penitence, provision is made for us to acknowledge our share in the plundering of natural resources and the spoiling of the natural world. Likewise, forms of Intercession are provided that focus on the theme of creation, and help us to bring before God the needs of the world at this time of ecological crisis. At the Dismissal, a form of corporate commitment is provided so that the whole congregation can express a desire to increase its awareness of the environment and strengthen its resolve to care for creation.

This Eucharist may be celebrated in the usual place of worship. But local churches are encouraged to consider arranging to have this celebration outside, either in a rural setting, or in a green space in an urban environment, according to the context of the local church.

The Gathering

The Greeting

We gather in praise of the God who is Father, Son and Holy Spirit.

All **Amen.**

This is the day that the Lord has made.

All **Let us rejoice and be glad in it.**

The Lord be with you

All **and also with you.**

Silence is kept.

All **Almighty God,**
to whom all hearts are open,
all desires known,
and from whom no secrets are hidden:
cleanse the thoughts of our hearts
by the inspiration of your holy Spirit,
that we may perfectly love you,
and worthily magnify your holy name;
through Christ our Lord.
Amen.

Prayers of Penitence

Let us confess our greed
and repent of the ways in which we have damaged God's
good creation:

We confess to you
our lack of care for the world you have given us.
Lord have mercy.

All **Lord have mercy.**

We confess to you
our selfishness in not sharing the earth's bounty fairly.
Christ have mercy.

All **Christ have mercy.**

We confess to you
our failure to protect the environment.
Lord have mercy.

All **Lord have mercy.**

The president declares God's forgiveness.

May the Father of all mercies
cleanse you from your sins,
and restore you in his image
to the praise and glory of his name,
through Jesus Christ our Lord.

All **Amen.**

The Gloria in excelsis may be used

All **Glory to God in the highest,**
and peace to his people on earth.
Lord God, heavenly King,
almighty God and Father,
we worship you, we give you thanks,
we praise you for your glory.
Lord Jesus Christ, only Son of the Father,
Lord God, Lamb of God,
you take away the sin of the world:
have mercy on us;
you are seated at the right hand of the Father:
receive our prayer.
For you alone are the Holy One,
you alone are the Lord,
you alone are the Most High, Jesus Christ,
with the Holy Spirit,
in the glory of God the Father.
Amen.

The Collect

In a time of silence,
let us pray that our worship will bring us closer to the one who
has created all things.

Glorious God,
the whole creation proclaims your marvellous work:
increase in us a capacity to wonder and delight in it,
that heaven's praise may echo in our hearts
and our lives be spent as good stewards of the earth,
through Jesus Christ our Lord.

All **Amen.**

The Liturgy of the Word

Reading(s)

Either one or two readings from Scripture on pages 99–100 precede the Gospel reading.

At the end of each the reader may say

This is the word of the Lord.

All **Thanks be to God.**

The psalm or canticle follows the first reading; other hymns and songs may be used between the readings. Alternatively the Lament on pages 44–45 may be used.

Gospel Reading

This acclamation may herald the Gospel reading.

Alleluia, alleluia.
You are worthy, our Lord and God,
to receive glory and honour and power,
for you created all things.

All **Alleluia.**

When the Gospel is announced the reader says

Hear the Gospel of our Lord Jesus Christ according to *N.*

All **Glory to you, O Lord.**

At the end

This is the Gospel of the Lord.

All **Praise to you, O Christ.**

Sermon

On Sundays and Principal Holy Days an authorized translation of the Nicene Creed is used, or on occasion the Apostles' Creed or an authorized Affirmation of Faith may be used.

All **We believe in one God,**
      the Father, the Almighty,
      maker of heaven and earth,
      of all that is,
      seen and unseen.
      We believe in one Lord, Jesus Christ,
      the only Son of God,
      eternally begotten of the Father,
      God from God, Light from Light,
      true God from true God,
      begotten, not made,
      of one Being with the Father;
      through him all things were made.
      For us and for our salvation he came down from heaven,
      was incarnate from the Holy Spirit and the Virgin Mary
      and was made man.
      For our sake he was crucified under Pontius Pilate;
      he suffered death and was buried.
      On the third day he rose again
      in accordance with the Scriptures;
      he ascended into heaven
      and is seated at the right hand of the Father.
      He will come again in glory to judge the living and the dead,
      and his kingdom will have no end.
      We believe in the Holy Spirit,
      the Lord, the giver of life,
      who proceeds from the Father and the Son,
      who with the Father and the Son is worshipped and glorified,
      who has spoken through the prophets.
      We believe in one holy catholic and apostolic Church.
      We acknowledge one baptism for the forgiveness of sins.
      We look for the resurrection of the dead,
      and the life of the world to come.
      Amen.

One of the forms on pages 65–72 may be used. This response may be used

    God of life:

All **hear our prayer.**

The prayers end

    Merciful Father,

All **accept these prayers**
    for the sake of your Son,
    our Saviour Jesus Christ.
    Amen.

The Liturgy of the Sacrament

The Peace

    You shall go out in joy and be led back in peace;
    the mountains and the hills before you shall burst into song,
    and all the trees of the field shall clap their hands.

    The peace of the Lord be always with you

All   **and also with you.**

    Let us offer one another a sign of peace.

All may exchange a sign of peace.

Preparation of the Table

Taking of the Bread and Wine

A hymn may be sung.

The gifts of the people may be gathered and presented.

The table is prepared and bread and wine are placed upon it.

This prayer at the preparation of the table may be said.

As the grain once scattered in the fields
and the grapes once dispersed on the hillside
are now united on this table in bread and wine,
so, Lord, may your whole Church soon be gathered together
from the corners of the earth
into your kingdom.

All **Amen.**

The president takes the bread and wine.

The Eucharistic Prayer (G)

The Lord be with you

All **and also with you.**

Lift up your hearts.

All **We lift them to the Lord.**

Let us give thanks to the Lord our God.

All **It is right to give thanks and praise.**

Blessed are you, Lord God,
our light and our salvation;
to you be glory and praise for ever.

From the beginning you have created all things
and all your works echo the silent music of your praise.
In the fullness of time you made us in your image,
the crown of all creation.

You give us breath and speech, that with angels and archangels
and all the powers of heaven
we may find a voice to sing your praise:

All **Holy, holy, holy Lord,**
God of power and might,
heaven and earth are full of your glory.
Hosanna in the highest.

Blessed is he who comes in the name of the Lord.
Hosanna in the highest.

How wonderful the work of your hands, O Lord.
As a mother tenderly gathers her children,
you embraced a people as your own.
When they turned away and rebelled
your love remained steadfast.

From them you raised up Jesus our Saviour, born of Mary,
to be the living bread,
in whom all our hungers are satisfied.
He offered his life for sinners,
and with a love stronger than death
he opened wide his arms on the cross.

On the night before he died,
he came to supper with his friends
and, taking bread, he gave you thanks.
He broke it and gave it to them, saying:
Take, eat; this is my body which is given for you;
do this in remembrance of me.

At the end of supper, taking the cup of wine,
he gave you thanks, and said:
Drink this, all of you; this is my blood of the new covenant,
which is shed for you and for many for the forgiveness of sins.
Do this, as often as you drink it, in remembrance of me.

Jesus Christ is Lord:

All **Lord, by your cross and resurrection**
you have set us free.
You are the Saviour of the world.

Father, we plead with confidence
his sacrifice made once for all upon the cross;
we remember his dying and rising in glory,
and we rejoice that he intercedes for us at your right hand.

Pour out your Holy Spirit as we bring before you
these gifts of your creation;
may they be for us the body and blood of your dear Son.

As we eat and drink these holy things in your presence,
form us in the likeness of Christ,
and build us into a living temple to your glory.

[Remember, Lord, your Church in every land.
Reveal her unity, guard her faith,
and preserve her in peace ...]

Bring us at the last with *[N and]* all the saints
to the vision of that eternal splendour
for which you have created us;
through Jesus Christ, our Lord,
by whom, with whom, and in whom,
with all who stand before you in earth and heaven,
we worship you, Father almighty, in songs of everlasting praise:

**All Blessing and honour and glory and power
be yours for ever and ever.
Amen.**

The Lord's Prayer

As our Saviour taught us, so we pray

**All Our Father in heaven,
hallowed be your name,
your kingdom come,
your will be done,
on earth as in heaven.
Give us today our daily bread.
Forgive us our sins
as we forgive those who sin against us.
Lead us not into temptation
but deliver us from evil.
For the kingdom, the power,
and the glory are yours
now and for ever.
Amen.**

Breaking of the Bread

The president breaks the consecrated bread

We break this bread
to share in the body of Christ.

**All Though we are many, we are one body,
because we all share in one bread.**

The Agnus Dei may be used as the bread is broken

All   **Jesus, Lamb of God, have mercy on us.**
      Jesus, bearer of our sins, have mercy on us.
      Jesus, redeemer of the world, grant us peace.

or

All   **Lamb of God, you take away the sin of the world,**
      have mercy on us.
      Lamb of God, you take away the sin of the world,
      have mercy on us.
      Lamb of God, you take away the sin of the world,
      grant us peace.

Giving of Communion

God's holy gifts
for God's holy people.

or

Draw near with faith

All   **Jesus Christ is holy,**
      Jesus Christ is Lord,
      to the glory of God the Father.

The president and people receive communion. Authorized words of distribution are used and the communicant replies Amen.

During the distribution hymns and anthems may be sung.

Prayer after Communion

Silence is kept.

Creator God,
send your Holy Spirit to renew this living world,
that the whole creation,
in its groaning and striving,
may know your loving purpose
and come to reflect your glory;
in Jesus Christ our Lord.

All   **Amen.**

The Dismissal

A hymn may be sung.

The following Act of Commitment may be used.

'While all creatures stand in expectation, what will be the result
of our liberty?'

(Thomas Traherne)

As the whole of creation looks with eager longing for the
redemption of humankind, let us pledge ourselves anew to serve
our Creator God, the Father who is the maker of all things, the Son
through whom all things are made, and the Holy Spirit, the giver
of life, who renews the face of the earth.

Let us stand to affirm our commitment to care actively for God's
creation.

**All   Lord of life and giver of hope,
we pledge ourselves to care for creation,
to reduce our waste,
to live sustainably,
and to value the rich diversity of life.
May your wisdom guide us,
that life in all its forms may flourish,
and may be faithful in voicing creation's praise.**

The president may use this or another suitable blessing (see page 75)

> May God the Father of our Lord Jesus Christ,
> the source of all goodness,
> pour his blessing upon all things created,
> and upon us his children,
> that we may use his gifts to his glory
> and the welfare of all peoples;
> and the blessing ...

A minister says

> Go in peace, and may the commitment we have made this day
> be matched by our faithful living.

All   Thanks be to God. Amen. Amen. Amen.

ALTERNATIVE AND SEASONAL MATERIAL

Invitations to Confession

1   Human sin disfigures the whole creation,
     which groans with eager longing for God's redemption.
     We confess our sin in penitence and faith.

2   As those who know the generosity of God,
     let us confess our sins,
     especially the ways in which we take creation and God's gifts
     for granted.

Kyrie Confessions

1   Lord, you delight in creation, its colour and diversity;
     yet we have misused the earth
     and plundered its resources for our own selfish ends.
     Lord, have mercy.
     Lord, have mercy.

     You have brought order out of chaos,
     light in darkness, good out of evil,
     but we have preferred darkness
     in words and deeds which dishonour God's holy name.
     Christ, have mercy.
     Christ, have mercy.

     You have showered us with blessings,
     but we have been grudging towards others
     and lacking in generosity in word and deed.
     Lord, have mercy.
     Lord, have mercy.

2   Lord, you give us this good earth,
     yet we take your generous gifts for granted.
     Lord, have mercy.
     Lord, have mercy.

     Lord, you give us this good earth,
     but we squander its rich resources.
     Christ, have mercy.
     Christ, have mercy.

Lord, you give us this good earth,
but we fail to share your bounty with all of your children.
Lord, have mercy.
Lord, have mercy.

3   God has blessed us,
but still God's children go hungry.
Lord, have mercy.
Lord, have mercy.

God has blessed us,
but still the poor cry out for justice.
Christ, have mercy.
Christ, have mercy.

God has blessed us,
but still we see inequality and oppression in the earth.
Lord, have mercy.
Lord, have mercy.

4   Lord, you give us seedtime and harvest,
forgive us for those times when we waste our food.
Lord, have mercy.
Lord, have mercy.

Lord, you make us one bread, one body,
forgive us when we fail to share the good things you give us.
Christ, have mercy.
Christ, have mercy.

Lord, you give us our daily bread,
may we hunger and thirst for you, the living bread.
Lord, have mercy.
Lord, have mercy.

Prayers of Penitence

1   We confess our sin, and the sins of our society,
in the misuse of God's creation.

God our Father, we are sorry
for the times when we have used your gifts carelessly,
and acted ungratefully.
Father, in your mercy:
forgive us and help us.

We enjoy the fruits of the harvest,
but sometimes forget that you have given them to us.
Father, in your mercy:
forgive us and help us.

We belong to a people who are full and satisfied,
but ignore the cry of the hungry.
Father, in your mercy:
forgive us and help us.

We are thoughtless,
and do not care enough for the environment and the world you
have made.
Father, in your mercy:
forgive us and help us.

2   Creator God, maker of heaven and earth,
we acknowledge our failure to live responsibly
as part of your creation.

We have taken what we want,
without considering the consequences;
we have wasted and discarded,
without thought for the future.
Open our hearts and minds to the signs of our times,
to the groaning of creation,
so that we may turn from our greed and lack of vision
and see a world being made anew in Jesus Christ our Lord.

All   **Amen.**

Collects

1   Almighty God,
    you have created the heavens and the earth
    and made us in your own image:
    teach us to discern your hand in all your works
    and your likeness in all your children;
    through Jesus Christ your Son our Lord,
    who with you and the Holy Spirit reigns supreme over all things,
    now and for ever.
    Amen.

2   Almighty God and Father,
    you have so ordered our life
    that we are dependent on one another:
    prosper those engaged in commerce and industry
    and direct their minds and hands
    that they may rightly use your gifts in the service of others;
    through Jesus Christ your Son our Lord,
    who is alive and reigns with you,
    in the unity of the Holy Spirit,
    one God, now and for ever.
    Amen.

3   Almighty God,
    whose will it is that the earth and the sea
        should bear their fruit in due season:
    bless the labours of those who work on land and sea,
    grant us a good harvest
    and the grace always to rejoice in your fatherly care;
    through Jesus Christ your Son our Lord,
    who is alive and reigns with you,
    in the unity of the Holy Spirit,
    one God, now and for ever.
    Amen.

4   God our Father,
    you never cease the work you have begun
    and prosper with your blessing all human labour:
    make us wise and faithful stewards of your gifts
    that we may serve the common good,
    maintain the fabric of our world
    and seek that justice where all may share
        the good things you pour upon us;
    through Jesus Christ your Son our Lord,
    who is alive and reigns with you,
    in the unity of the Holy Spirit,
    one God, now and for ever.
    Amen.

5   Eternal God,
    you crown the year with your goodness
    and you give us the fruits of the earth in their season:
    grant that we may use them to your glory,
    for the relief of those in need and for our own well-being;
    through Jesus Christ your Son our Lord,
    who is alive and reigns with you,
    in the unity of the Holy Spirit,
    one God, now and for ever.
    Amen.

Gospel Acclamations

1   Alleluia, alleluia.
    God has spoken to us through his Son,
    through whom he created all things.
    Alleluia.

2   Alleluia, alleluia.
    The sower sows the seed, which is the word of the Lord:
    Those who accept it bear fruit, thirty and sixty and a
    hundredfold.' *(cf Mark 4.3,8,20)*
    Alleluia.

3 Alleluia, alleluia.
We do not live by bread alone,
but by every word that comes from the mouth of God.
Alleluia.

4 Alleluia, alleluia.
As the rain and the snow come down from heaven and water
the earth
making it spring forth and grow,
so shall my word accomplish my purpose.
Alleluia.

Intercessions

1 In peace let us pray to the Father, through the Son
and in the power of the Holy Spirit, who make, sustain and
renew all things.
Heavenly Father,
we pray for your Church throughout the world
that we may be faithful to our baptism.
With the dawn of each day,
may we be awakened to the beauty of the earth
and rejoice in the wonder and diversity of creation in all its forms
and colour.
Lord, hear us.
Lord, graciously hear us.

Lord of life,
as all living things depend on the good quality
of the air, the soil, and water,
may your wisdom guide us as we care for the environment.
Deliver us from selfishness and rapacious greed.
Help us to share the rich resources of this world gladly and justly,
in the cause of stability and peace between nations and peoples.
Lord, hear us.
Lord, graciously hear us.

Lord of mercy,
we bring before you areas affected by chronic shortage of water,
and pray for those suffering as a result of drought
or the lack of safe water to drink.
We pray for those suffering from the effects of extreme weather
and whose environment has been damaged
by cyclones, floods or destructive wildfires.
May we better understand the effects
of the changing patterns of weather on our planet.
Lord, hear us.
Lord, graciously hear us.

Lord of abundant life,
we give thanks for the rich harvest of the seas;
may we cherish the good things you have created
and be successful in reducing the pollution
in our oceans, rivers and lakes that life may flourish.
May your wisdom help us to maintain the biodiversity of our
    fragile planet.
Strengthen our resolve and bless the efforts of all
who seek to protect the marine, animal, insect and plant life
that are threatened with extinction.
Lord, hear us.
Lord, graciously hear us.

Lord of creation,
you have placed us on the earth to care for it,
and call us to be co-workers with Christ your Son.
Bless our farmers, those who work in our nature reserves and
    National Parks,
in our Areas of Outstanding Natural Beauty and Sites of
    Scientific Interest.
and all who are custodians of our landscape.
Lord, hear us.
Lord, graciously hear us.

Lord of the universe,
you have made us from the stuff of the earth,
and to earth we shall return.
May we tread lightly upon this earth
and succeed in the innovation and development
of sources of renewable energy and green technology.
By your grace, may we live our days wisely,
live sustainably,
and at the last come with all your saints
into paradise and enjoy creation made new.

Merciful Father,
accept these prayers
for the sake of your Son
our Saviour, Jesus Christ.
Amen.

2   Let us pray to God the almighty, the Lord of creation.

God said, 'Let there be light.'
Eternal God, we thank you for your light and your truth.
We praise you for your wisdom and power
in creating this universe which proclaims your glory.
Inspire us to worship you, the creator of all,
and let your light shine upon our world.
God of life:
hear our prayer.

God said, 'Let there be a firmament in the midst of the heavens.'
We thank you for the vastness of the universe
and the mysteries of space.
We pray for all scientists and astronomers
who extend the boundaries of our knowledge.
As we contemplate the wonder of the heavens,
confirm us in the truth that every human being is
    known and loved by you.
God of life:
hear our prayer.

God said, 'Let the waters be gathered together,
and let dry land appear.'
We thank you for the beauty of the earth,
for the diversity of land and sea,
for the resources of the earth.
Give us the will to safeguard this planet
and to use its riches for the good and welfare of all.
God of life:
hear our prayer.

God said, 'Let there be lights in the sky
to separate the day and the night.'
We thank you for the warmth of the sun,
the light of the moon, the glory of the stars.
We praise you for the formations of clouds,
the radiance of dawn and sunset.
Forgive us wasting or abusing the energy
    on which all life depends.
Open our eyes to behold your beauty,
and our lips to praise your name.
God of life:
hear our prayer.

God said, 'Let the waters bring forth living creatures,
and let birds fly across the sky.'
We thank you for the teeming life of the seas,
and the flight of the birds.
Help us to protect the environment
so that all life may flourish.
God of life:
hear our prayer.

God said, 'Let us create human beings in our own image.'
We pray for the human family.
We rejoice in its diversity,
we repent of its divisions and violence.
By the power of your Spirit, restore your image in us,
through Christ who came to remake us
by his death and resurrection.
God of life:
hear our prayer.

Heavenly Father, you have filled the world with beauty:
open our eyes to behold your gracious hand in all your works;
that, rejoicing in your whole creation,
we may learn to serve you with gladness;
for the sake of him through whom all things were made,
your Son Jesus Christ our Lord.
Amen.

3   Let us pray to God,
    that he will bring to fruition all that he desires
        for his creation.
    Father, Lord of creation,
    in your mercy, hear us.

You have created the universe by your eternal Word,
and have blessed humankind in making us
        stewards of the earth.
We pray for your world,
that we may share and conserve its resources,
and live in reverence for the creation
and in harmony with one another.
Father, Lord of creation,
in your mercy, hear us.

You have given the human race a rich land,
a land of streams and springs,
wheat and barley,
vines and oil and honey.
We have made by sin a world of suffering and sorrow.
We pray for those who bear the weight of affliction
that they may come to share the life of wholeness
        and plenty.
Father, Lord of creation,
in your mercy, hear us.

In Christ you call us to a new way of life,
loving our neighbours before ourselves.
Help us to treat with care and respect the world as it is
as we live in hope and anticipation of the world
        as it will be
when your kingdom comes and your will is done.
Father, Lord of creation,
in your mercy, hear us.

We thank you for those, living and departed,
who have shown a true respect for your creation ...
Help us to follow in their footsteps,
until, with them, we see you face to face,
where all is made new in Christ our Lord.
Merciful Father,
accept these prayers
for the sake of your Son
our Saviour, Jesus Christ.
Amen.

4   Let us ask the God of Creation to send a blessing upon us.

Upon the rich earth send a blessing, O Lord.
Let the earth be fruitful
and its resources be hallowed.
We ask in faith:
Hear us, good Lord.

Upon human labour send a blessing, O Lord.
Prosper the work of our hands;
may all find dignity and just reward in their work;
free the exploited and oppressed.
We ask in faith:
Hear us, good Lord.

Upon the produce of the earth send a blessing, O Lord.
Guide us into a sustainable future,
and give us the will to share the fruits of the world.
We ask in faith:
Hear us, good Lord.

Upon the seas and waters send a blessing, O Lord.
Teach us to cherish the water of the earth,
and to conserve the seas, lakes and rivers.
We ask in faith:
Hear us, good Lord.

Upon aid agencies send a blessing, O Lord.
Where the earth is parched and the well has run dry;
where war brings want, and children go hungry;
where the poor cry out for bread and for justice,
give hands to care and heal, and compel us to be generous.
We ask in faith:
Hear us, good Lord.

We ask you to hear us, good Lord,
for the sake of your Son,
our Saviour Jesus Christ.
Amen.

5   Let us offer our prayers to God for the life of the world
and for all God's people in their daily life and work.
God, the beginning and end of all things,
in your providence and care
you watch unceasingly over all creation;
we offer our prayers
that in us and in all your people your will may be done,
according to your wise and loving purpose in Christ our Lord.
Lord of life:
hear our prayer.

We pray for all engaged in research to safeguard crops
        against disease,
and to produce abundant life among those who hunger
and whose lives are at risk.
Prosper the work of their hands
and the searching of their minds,
that their labour may be for the welfare of all.
Lord of wisdom:
hear our prayer.

We pray for governments and aid agencies,
and those areas of the world affected by climate change.
By the grace of your Spirit,
touch our hearts
and the hearts of all who live in comfortable plenty,
and make us wise stewards of your gifts.
Lord of justice:
hear our prayer.

We offer ourselves to your service,
asking that by the Spirit at work in us
others may receive a rich harvest of love and joy and peace.
Lord of faithfulness:
hear our prayer.

God of grace,
as you are ever at work in your creation,
so fulfil your wise and loving purpose in us
and in all for whom we pray,
that with them and in all that you have made,
your glory may be revealed
and the whole earth give praise to you,
through Jesus Christ our Lord.
Amen.

Prayers at the Preparation of the Table

1   Blessed be God,
    by whose grace creation is renewed,
    by whose love heaven is opened,
    by whose mercy we offer our sacrifice of praise.
    Blessed be God for ever.

2   Blessed are you, Lord God of all creation:
    through your goodness we have this bread to set before you,
    which earth has given and human hands have made.
    It will become for us the bread of life.
    Blessed be God for ever.

Blessed are you, Lord God of all creation:
through your goodness we have this wine to set before you,
fruit of the vine and work of human hands.
It will become for us the cup of salvation.
Blessed be God for ever.

3   Blessed are you, Lord God of all creation;
you bring forth bread from the earth.
Blessed be God for ever.

Blessed are you, Lord God of all creation;
you create the fruit of the vine.
Blessed be God for ever.

Eucharistic Prefaces

1   And now we give you thanks
because in him, our risen Lord,
the new creation is being brought to perfection,
a broken world is being renewed,
and creation itself will share
in the glorious liberty of the children of God.

2   And now we give you thanks
for your ancient promise
that while the earth endures,
seedtime and harvest, cold and heat,
summer and winter, day and night,
will never cease.

3   And now we give you thanks
because all things are of your making,
all times and seasons obey your laws,
but you have chosen to create us in your own image,
setting us over the whole world in all its wonder.
You have made us stewards of your creation,
to praise you day by day
for the marvels of your wisdom and power:
so earth unites with heaven
to sing the new song of creation:
Holy, holy, holy Lord ...

The following prefaces are for use with Additional Eucharistic Prayer (2)
'on occasions when a significant number of children are present'.[8]

4   You give us sun and moon and star-lit sky,
     everything that gives us light,
     light for our eyes, our hearts, our minds.

5   You give us the fish in the sea,
     the birds of the air,
     and every plant and tree;
     the life that sleeps in the winter earth,
     and awakens again in the spring.

Post Communions

1   God our creator,
     by your gift
     the tree of life was set at the heart of the earthly paradise,
     and the bread of life at the heart of your Church:
     may we who have been nourished at your table on earth
     be transformed by the glory of the Saviour's cross
     and enjoy the delights of eternity;
     through Jesus Christ our Lord.
     Amen.

2   God our creator,
     you give us seed to sow and bread to eat:
     as you have blessed the fruit of our labour in this eucharist,
     so we ask you to give all your children their daily bread,
     that the world may praise you for your goodness;
     through Jesus Christ our Lord.
     Amen.

3   Lord of the harvest,
     with joy we have offered thanksgiving for your love in creation
     and have shared in the bread and the wine of the kingdom:
     by your grace plant within us a reverence for all that you give us
     and make us generous and wise stewards
          of the good things we enjoy;
     through Jesus Christ our Lord.
     Amen.

---

[8] *Common Worship: Additional Eucharistic Prayers with Guidance on Celebrating the Eucharist with Children, CHP, © Archbishops' Council 2012 p.1*

Blessings

1   May God the Father,
     who clothes the lilies of the field
     and feeds the birds of the air,
     provide you with all we need for life in its fullness.
     Amen.

     May God the Son,
     who fed the five thousand and turned water into wine,
     feed you with his life and transform us in his love.
     Amen.

     May God the Holy Spirit,
     who hovered over the waters of creation
     and formed the world from chaos,
     form you in the likeness of Christ and renew the face of the earth.
     Amen.

     And the blessing …

2   May God
     who clothes the lilies of the field and feeds the birds of the air,
     who leads the lambs to pasture and the deer to water,
     who multiplied loaves and fishes, and changed water into wine,
     lead us and feed us,
     and change us to reflect the glory of our Creator
     now and through all eternity;
     and the blessing …

Dismissals and Endings

1   Tend the earth, care for God's good creation,
     and bring forth the fruits of righteousness.
     Go in the peace of Christ.
     Thanks be to God.

2   Freely you have received, freely give.
     Go in peace to love and serve the Lord.
     In the name of Christ. Amen.

A SEASON OF CREATION:
Thematic resources for use over four weeks

These three strands of thematic resources can be used during the Season of Creation in September and early October, or at other points during the year when a church community wishes to focus on creation and environmental themes. If used in September this may be enriched by an observance of the Feast of the Holy Cross (page 101) and come to focus either at Harvest Festival or the Feast of St Francis of Assisi (page 104).

Strand 1 – Of Every Kind

This is based on the four annual observances resourced by 'Seasons and Festivals of the Agricultural Year' in *Common Worship: Times and Seasons*. These four times of the year reflect the life-giving process of sowing seed, caring for the growing crops, harvesting, eating and storing them. During the Season of Creation this natural process might be the focus of four weeks of reflection.

Blessed are you, Lord God of all creation:

All **For in your abundant care you have given us fertile land.**

Collect

Ever living God,
you created the earth
which gives us its food in due season;
give us the will to cherish the earth
and to use its riches for the good and welfare of all people.
This we ask through Jesus Christ our Lord.

All Amen.

Week 1: Sowing	Week 2: Growing	Week 3: Gathering	Week 4: Treasuring
Based on Plough Sunday	Based on Rogationtide	Based on Lammastide	Based on Harvest
Genesis 1.9–13	Ezekiel 47.[1–6a] 6b–12	Leviticus 23.9–14	Deuteronomy 26.1–11
Psalm 104.1,6,11–26	Psalm 147.1–13; Benedicite	Psalm 126	Psalm 65
2 Corinthians 9.9–11a	Philippians 4.4–7	James 5.7–9	Colossians 1.1–15
Matthew 6.25–34 or Matthew 13.1–9	Matthew 6.7–15 or John 12.23–26	Matthew 15.32–39 or John 4.31–38	Luke 12.16–30

Strand 2 – The Garden

This is based on the agricultural year themes in *Common Worship: Times and Seasons* but in a form that may be more readily accessible to people living in less rural situations, by children (e.g. in schools or congregations where there is a large proportion of children) and perhaps by those less familiar with church.

Blessed are you, Lord God of all creation:

All For you give us the fruits of the earth in their season.

Collect

Lord of all life,
you created the universe,
and gave us this beautiful earth
to discover and to cherish;
help us to wonder at creation,
to treasure your gifts
and to use them to your glory.

All   Amen.   *(cf Additional Eucharistic Prayers: Prayer 2)*

Week 1: The Spade	Week 2: The Watering Can	Week 3: The Basket	Week 4: The Plate

Genesis
  1.9–13, 29–31
	Joel 2.21–27 *or*
	Song of Songs
	  2.10–13 *or*
	Isaiah 55.10–13 *or*
	Ezekiel
	  47.[1–6a] 6b–12
		Deuteronomy
		  26.1–11
			Isaiah 55.1–2

Psalm 126	Psalm 65.8–13	Psalm 104.1,29–32	Psalm 107
			Acts 2.43–47
Matthew 13.1–9 *or* Matthew 13.31–33	Luke 13.6–9	Mark 4.26–32	Matthew 15.32–39 *or* John 21.1–14 *or* Luke 14.15–23(24)

Strand 3 – Creation Emergency

This offers a way to address the climate and environmental emergency
directly within the context of an understanding of Creation as a gift.
Over the four weeks of the Season of Creation the readings reflect on the
wonder and abundance of creation, the damage that is wreaked upon it
and the desire and hope for healing.

Blessed are you, Lord God of all creation,
with you is the well of life:

All   And in your light shall we see light.

Collect

God our Creator,
who laid the foundations of the earth
and stretched out the heavens as a tent cloth;
how glorious is your name in all the world.
Give us grace to wonder at your gift,
to treasure the earth
and to work for its protection and renewal;
through Jesus Christ your Son, our Lord,
who is alive and reigns with you,
in the unity of the Holy Spirit,
one God, now and for ever.

All Amen.

Week 1: Wonder	Week 2: Abundance	Week 3: Desolation	Week 4: Restoration
Job 38.1–11,16-18 or Proverbs 8.1–4,22–31	Deuteronomy 8.7–18	Isaiah 5.1–10 or Jeremiah 14.1–21	Genesis 8.12–20 or Genesis 9.8–17 or Job 42.10-17
Psalm 33 or Psalm 89 Ecclesiasticus 42.15–33	Psalm 19; Benedicite	Psalm 102	Psalm 126
Colossians 1.1–15	Revelation 22.1–5	Revelation 6.12–17	Romans 8.18–22
John 1.1–14	Matthew 6.25–34	Mark 11.12–20 or Matthew 24.15–28	Mark 4.30–32 or John 6.1–13

SEASONS AND FESTIVALS OF THE AGRICULTURAL YEAR

Introduction

The Jewish and Christian Scriptures give eloquent expression to the creative power and wisdom of God. It is therefore a natural instinct for worshipping communities to develop patterns of worship and prayer around the agricultural year. Of course, there were dangers, and the same Scriptures bear witness to concerns about the idolatry of fertility cults and the worship of created things rather than the creator. Nevertheless, ancient society lived close to the land, and it is no surprise that the ancient Jewish festivals of Passover and Unleavened Bread, Weeks and Tabernacles all have agrarian roots. The Christian tradition, too, has assimilated, but with differing emphases and in different times and places, particular agricultural festivals. Much of this is bound up with the need to provide food to sustain human life, and the accompanying sense of a proper humility before God as source of all things, gratitude for his goodness, and responsibility in stewarding the resources of the earth. In more recent years, urban congregations have explored ways of adapting traditional creation-based festivals for their own contexts.[9] This provision is not intended to limit such adaptation.

Plough Sunday

The observance of Plough Sunday on the First Sunday of Epiphany goes back to Victorian times, but behind it there is a much older observance, associated with the first working day after the twelve days of Christmas, hence 'Plough Monday' in some places. In days when work was scarce in winter, the observance looked forward to the time of sowing with the promise of a harvest to come. Some Christian communities have reintroduced it as a focus for asking a blessing on human labour near the start of the calendar year.

Forms are provided here for the blessing of a plough and the blessing of seed. Lectionary material is also provided.

---

[9] See ideas in, for example, *Creative Ideas for Wild Church: Taking all-age worship and learning outdoors* and *Together for a Season: All-age resources for Feasts and Festivals of the Christian Year* (details in Appendix)

Rogationtide

The Rogation Days (from the Latin *rogare*, 'to ask') are the three weekdays before Ascension Day. However, in practice, many churches have observed Rogation on the preceding Sunday (Easter V in the Prayer Book, the Sixth Sunday of Easter in *Common Worship*). The Prayer Book Gospel includes the words of Jesus, 'Whatsoever ye shall ask for in my Name, he will give it you' – words associated with the heavenly intercession of the ascended Christ.

Originally, the Christian observance of Rogation was taken over from Graeco-Roman religion, where an annual procession invoked divine favour to protect crops against mildew. The tradition grew of using processional litanies, often around the parish boundaries, for the blessing of the land. These processions concluded with a mass. The Rogation procession was suppressed at the Reformation, but it was restored in 1559. The poet George Herbert interpreted the procession as a means of asking for God's blessing on the land, of preserving boundaries, of encouraging fellowship between neighbours with the reconciling of differences, and of charitable giving to the poor. The tradition of 'beating the bounds' has been preserved in some communities, while others maintain the traditional use of the Litany within worship. In more recent times, the scope of Rogation has been widened to include petition for the world of work and for accountable stewardship, and prayer for local communities, whether rural or urban.

The provision here includes resource material for Rogationtide worship, litanies for the Rogationtide procession, and patterns of readings. The material is to be used with flexibility according to local circumstances.

Lammastide

Lammas or 'Loaf-mass' (derived from the Anglo-Saxon *Hlafmaesse*) is an English feast in origin, held on 1 August as a thanksgiving for the first-fruits of the wheat harvest. Traditionally, a newly baked loaf from the wheat harvest was presented before God within the mass of that day. While the ceremony ceased at the Reformation, reference to Lammas Day continued in the Prayer Book calendar, and the practice has been revived in some places in more recent years. The tradition of giving thanks for the first-fruits need not be limited to 1 August, and churches are at liberty to decide when to hold such a celebration. Here, material is provided to form the Gathering rite of the eucharist. The Lammas loaf should ideally be baked by members of the congregation, using local produce wherever possible. Other small loaves or buns, in the tradition of 'blessed bread', may be distributed to the congregation. Part of the Lammas loaf may be used as the eucharistic bread on this occasion. Two patterns of readings are suggested, the first concerning the offering of the first-fruits and the second concerning the bread of life.

Harvest

Harvest Thanksgiving is a more modern addition to the church calendar. Its origins are usually traced to the adaptation in 1843 of Lammas Day by the Revd R. S. Hawker, a parish priest in Cornwall. He chose the first Sunday in October as a Christian response to coincide with the traditional but largely secular 'harvest home' celebration, but there is some evidence to suggest that a thanksgiving for the harvest was already a relatively widespread practice. An annual church celebration of the harvest certainly established itself rapidly with great popularity and was first recognized officially in the Church of England in 1862. Since then, many local traditions for the celebration have developed and many liturgical resources are available. Here, a bank of resource material is provided for use at Holy Communion or a Service of the Word. An Act of Thanksgiving is provided, which may accompany the tradition of bringing to church gifts of fresh produce and other foodstuffs.

Plough Sunday

The Blessing of the Plough & the Blessing of Seed

Note

Forms of prayer are provided for the blessing of a plough and the blessing of seed, along with lectionary provision. The material can be incorporated into Holy Communion or a Service of the Word. Other resource material from Seasons and Festivals of the Agricultural Year may be used or adapted appropriately.

The Blessing of the Plough or Drill

Blessed are you, Lord God of all creation:
for in your abundant care you have given us fertile land,
rich soil, the seasons in their courses.
You provide seed for sowing, water, light and warmth
to bring forth the miracle of growth.
You give us skill to work the land,
to prepare and nourish it, that it may be fruitful.
By your blessing,
let this plough be a sign of all that you promise to us.
Prosper the work of our hands,
and provide abundant crops for your people to share.
Blessed be God, Father, Son and Holy Spirit.
Blessed be God for ever.

God speed the plough.
God speed the plough.

The Blessing of Seed

Blessed are you, Lord God of all creation:
in your goodness you have given us this seed to sow.
In it we perceive the promise of life,
the wonders of your creative love.
By your blessing,
let this seed be for us a sign of your creative power,
that in sowing and watering,
tending and watching,
we may see the miracle of growth,
and in due course reap a rich harvest.

As this seed must die to give life,
reveal to us the saving power of your Son,
who died that we might live,
and plant in us the good seed of your word.
Blessed be God, Father, Son and Holy Spirit.
Blessed be God for ever.

By itself the earth produces:
first the stalk, then the ear, then the full grain shall appear.

The Collect

Almighty God and Father,
you have so ordered our life
that we are dependent on one another:
prosper those engaged in commerce and industry
and direct their minds and hands
that they may rightly use your gifts in the service of others;
through Jesus Christ your Son our Lord,
who is alive and reigns with you,
in the unity of the Holy Spirit,
one God, now and for ever.
All **Amen.**

Readings

Genesis 1.9–13 *or* Genesis 8.20—9.3 *or* Isaiah 55.6–11 *or*
    Ecclesiasticus 38.25–end
Psalm 37.22–38 *or* Psalm 104
1 Corinthians 9.6–14
Matthew 6.25–end

Rogation

The Rogationtide Procession

Note

This may be a procession within the church building or in the open air, whether the traditional beating of the bounds or a specified procession in part of the parish. Prayers and readings may be used at suitable places; in urban parishes, these might include street corners, parks and open spaces, and commercial or industrial sites.

The following resources may be used according to circumstances.

A

All or parts of the following litany may be said or sung

I

Let us pray.

God the Father, Lord of creation,
have mercy upon us.

God the Son, through whom all things were made,
have mercy upon us.

God the Holy Spirit, who renews the face of the earth,
have mercy upon us.

Holy, blessed and glorious Trinity, creating and saving God,
have mercy upon us.

Remember, Lord, your mercy and loving-kindness towards us.
Bless this good earth, and make it fruitful.
Bless our labour, and give us all things needful for our daily lives.
Bless the homes of this parish and all who live within them.
Bless our common life and our care for our neighbour.
Hear us, good Lord.

II

For all cities, towns and villages,
and for their well-being and prosperity,
let us pray to the Lord.
Lord, have mercy.

For the rural economy and for its regeneration,
let us pray to the Lord.
Lord, have mercy.

For those who tend the countryside
and preserve its order and beauty,
let us pray to the Lord.
Lord, have mercy.

For traditional rural skills and crafts
and for those who exercise them,
let us pray to the Lord.
Lord, have mercy.

For all farms, all who work them,
and for the whole farming industry,
let us pray to the Lord.
Lord, have mercy.

For those who make farming policy,
and for all with authority in government,
let us pray to the Lord.
Lord, have mercy.

III

For a blessing on our land we pray.
Hear us, good Lord.

For healthy crops and abundant harvests we pray.
Hear us, good Lord.

For the care and welfare of animals
and for the veterinary profession we pray.
Hear us, good Lord.

For the harvest of the soil
and for the fruits of the earth in their seasons we pray.
Hear us, good Lord.

For seasonable weather we pray.
Hear us, good Lord.

For protection from blight, pestilence and disease we pray.
Hear us, good Lord.

For those engaged in agricultural research we pray.
Hear us, good Lord.

For the service industries that support rural life we pray.
Hear us, good Lord.

For the ministry of your Church in rural areas we pray.
Hear us, good Lord.

For parts of the world where the harvests have failed we pray.
Hear us, good Lord.

For charities, aid agencies and overseas development we pray.
Hear us, good Lord.

IV

For our daily bread:
we pray to you, O Lord.

For all who work on the land to bring us our food in due season:
we pray to you, O Lord.

For all who fish the rivers, lakes and seas:
we pray to you, O Lord.

For all who process foods and prepare them for distribution and sale:
we pray to you, O Lord.

For all supermarkets and shops, and for all who work in them:
we pray to you, O Lord.

For those who work in food research:
we pray to you, O Lord.

For those who distribute food to those in need:
we pray to you, O Lord.

For the will to share your bounteous gifts:
we pray to you, O Lord.

V

For the world of work in all its diversity:
hear us, good Lord.

For the industry and workplaces of this *parish/community*:
hear us, good Lord.

For the right ordering of work in time of technological change:
hear us, good Lord.

For communities that have lost traditional industries,
and for their regeneration:
hear us, good Lord.

For all expanding industries and for the promise of new jobs:
hear us, good Lord.

For small businesses and co-operatives:
hear us, good Lord.

For local trade and commerce:
hear us, good Lord.

For all service industries that provide for our daily needs:
hear us, good Lord.

For the unemployed and for those living in poverty:
hear us, good Lord.

For school leavers and all who are seeking to enter employment:
hear us, good Lord.

For the retired and those unable to work:
hear us, good Lord.

For all who work as volunteers:
hear us, good Lord.

VI

Almighty and everlasting God,
you are always more ready to hear than we to pray
and to give more than either we desire or deserve:
pour down upon us the abundance of your mercy,
forgiving us those things of which our conscience is afraid
and giving us those good things
    which we are not worthy to ask
but through the merits and mediation
of Jesus Christ your Son our Lord.
Amen.

B

Collect

Almighty God,
whose will it is that the earth and the sea
    should bear their fruit in due season:
bless the labours of those who work on land and sea,
grant us a good harvest
and the grace always to rejoice in your fatherly care;
through Jesus Christ your Son our Lord,
who is alive and reigns with you,
in the unity of the Holy Spirit,
one God, now and for ever.
Amen.

*The following readings may be used at suitable points in the
procession. A selection may be made from either Table A or Table B,
according to circumstances. Suitable hymns or songs may be used in
place of the psalmody.*

A		**B**
1 Deuteronomy 26.1–11	Psalm 147.1–12	Genesis 8.13–end
2 Job 38.1–11,16–18	Psalm 104.25–end	Leviticus 26.1–13
3 Ezekiel 47.[1–6] 7–12	Psalm 107.23–32	Deuteronomy 8.1–10
4 Ecclesiasticus 38.27–32	Psalm 107.1–9	Hosea 2.18–end
5 Acts 14.8–18	Psalm 107.33–end	James 4.7–11
6 2 Corinthians 9.9–11a	Psalm 112	Romans 8.18–25
7 Philippians 4.4–7	Benedicite	1 Corinthians 3.10–14
8 Mark 11.22–24		John 6.22–40
or Matthew 6.7–15		*or* John 12.23–26

Lammas

The Presentation of the Lammas Loaf

Note

As the word 'Lammas' suggests, the setting for this material is the Holy Communion. the Lammas loaf, or part of it, may be used as the bread of the Eucharist, or the Lammas loaf and the eucharistic bread may be kept separate. To avoid any possible confusion, the rite of the presentation of the Lammas loaf should form part of the Gathering in Holy Communion Order One. Suitable patterns of readings are suggested.

The Gathering

At the entry of the ministers a hymn may be sung.

The president may say

> In the name of the Father,
> and of the Son,
> and of the Holy Spirit.
All Amen.

The Greeting

The president greets the people

> The Lord be with you
All And also with you.

The Presentation of the Lammas Loaf

The president introduces the service with these or other suitable words

Brothers and sisters in Christ, the people of God in ancient times presented to the Lord an offering of first-fruits as a sign of their dependence upon God for their daily bread. At this Lammastide, we bring a newly baked loaf as our offering in thanksgiving to God for his faithfulness.

Jesus said, 'I am the bread of life; those who come to me shall never be hungry and those who believe in me shall never thirst.' *John 6.35*

The Lammas loaf is brought to the president.

> Blessed are you, Lord God of all creation;
> you bring forth bread from the fields
> and give us the fruits of the earth in their seasons.
> Accept this loaf, which we bring before you,
> made from the harvest of your goodness.
> Let it be for us a sign of your fatherly care.
> Blessed are you, Lord our God,
> worthy of our thanksgiving and praise.

All Blessed be God for ever.

The service continues with the Prayers of Penitence.

The following Kyrie may be used

> Lord, you give us seedtime and harvest,
> forgive us for those times when we waste our food.
> Lord, have mercy.

All Lord, have mercy.

> Lord, you make us one bread, one body,
> We are sorry that we fail to share the good things you give us.
> Christ, have mercy.

All Christ have mercy.

> Lord, you provide our daily bread,
> may we hunger and thirst for you, the living bread.
> Lord, have mercy,

All Lord, have mercy.

Readings

The Offering of First-fruits
Leviticus 23.9–14
Psalm 126
1 Corinthians 15.12–20 *or* James 5.7–9
Matthew 15.32–39 *or* John 4.31–38

The Bread of Life
Exodus 16.11–15
Psalm 104.10–15
2 Corinthians 9.6–11
John 6.28–35

God our Father,
you never cease the work you have begun
and prosper with your blessing all human labour:
make us wise and faithful stewards of your gifts
that we may serve the common good,
maintain the fabric of our world
and seek that justice where all may share
     the good things you pour upon us;
through Jesus Christ your Son our Lord,
who is alive and reigns with you,
in the unity of the Holy Spirit,
one god, now and for ever.
Amen.

Harvest

Thanksgiving for the Harvest &
The Bringing Forward of Symbols of the Harvest

Thanksgiving for the Harvest

Let us give thanks to God,
the God of all peoples of the earth.

For the colour and forms of your creation
and our place within it,
we bring our thanks, good Lord:
your mercy endures for ever.

For our daily food,
and for those whose work and skill
bring your good gifts to us,
we bring our thanks, good Lord:
your mercy endures for ever.

For the gifts and graces inspired in human minds and hearts;
for insight and imagination,
for the skills of research
which bring healing and fulfilment to the lives of many;
we bring our thanks, good Lord:
your mercy endures for ever.

For the light and shades of the changing seasons,
and their variety and dependability;
for new life and growth out of barrenness and decay;
we bring our thanks, good Lord:
your mercy endures for ever.

For new hope and strength in our communities,
especially in your Church and among all you call to serve you,
we bring our thanks, good Lord:
your mercy endures for ever.

For all in whose lives we see
goodness, kindness, gentleness, patience and humility,
and all the fruit of the Spirit,
we bring our thanks, good Lord:
your mercy endures for ever.

For the life we have been given,
and for all those whom you have given us to share it,
we bring our thanks, good Lord:
your mercy endures for ever.

The Bringing Forward of Symbols of the Harvest

Let us bring forward symbols of the harvest,
gifts that God has created and his sun and rain have nurtured.
Thanks be to God.

Bring forward the harvest of the cornfields,
the oats and the wheat, the rye and the barley.
Thanks be to God.

Bring forward the harvest of roots,
the swedes and mangolds, turnips and sugar beet.
Thanks be to God.

Bring forward the harvest of seeds for next year's crops,
for clover, for hay and for corn.
Thanks be to God.

Bring forward the harvest of vegetables,
peas, potatoes, beans and hops.
Thanks be to God.

Bring forward the harvest of pears and apples, berries and herbs.
Thanks be to God.

Bring forward the harvest of flowers,
the finest blooms from our gardens and our fields.
Thanks be to God.

Bring forward the grain and the grape,
for our Saviour took bread and wine
to feed us with his body and his blood,
given and shed for the life of the world.
Let us feed on him by faith with thanksgiving.
Thanks be to God.

**Praise God, from whom all blessings flow,
praise him, all creatures here below,
praise him above, ye heavenly host,
praise Father, Son, and Holy Ghost.
Amen.**

Collect

Eternal God,
you crown the year with your goodness
and you give us the fruits of the earth in their season:
grant that we may use them to your glory,
for the relief of those in need and for our own well-being;
through Jesus Christ your Son our Lord,
who is alive and reigns with you,
in the unity of the Holy Spirit,
one God, now and for ever.
Amen.

OTHER RESOURCES

Acclamations

1   Where were you when I laid the foundations of the earth
and established its boundaries?
Lord, your purpose stands for ever.

Where were you when the morning stars sang together
and all the heavenly beings shouted for joy?
Lord, your purpose stands for ever.

Who shut up the sea behind doors
when it burst forth from the womb,
when I made the clouds its garment?
Lord, your purpose stands for ever.

Have you commanded the morning
and caused the dawn to know its place?
Lord, your purpose stands for ever.

From whose womb does the ice come forth
and who gives birth to the hoar-frost of heaven?
Lord, your purpose stands for ever.

Who has endowed the heart with wisdom,
and given understanding to the mind?
Lord, your purpose stands for ever.

2   God be gracious to us and bless us;
and make his face to shine upon us.

That your way may be known upon earth,
your saving power among all nations.

**Let the peoples praise you, O God;
let all the peoples praise you.**

O let the nations rejoice and be glad,
for you will judge the peoples righteously
    and govern the nations upon earth.

**Let the peoples praise you, O God;
let all the peoples praise you.**

Then shall the earth bring forth her increase,
and God, our own God, will bless us.
God will bless us,
and all the ends of the earth shall fear him.

Let the peoples praise you, O God;
let all the peoples praise you.

3   **The earth has yielded its harvest;**
      God, our God, has blessed us.

You visit the earth and water it;
you make it very plenteous.

You soften the ground with showers;
and bless the increase of it.

You crown the year with your goodness;
and your paths overflow with plenty.

The meadows are clothed with sheep;
the valleys stand so thick with corn,
they shout for joy and sing.

The earth has yielded its harvest;
God, our God, has blessed us.

Psalm Prayers

8   We bless you, master of the heavens,
for the wonderful order which enfolds this world;
grant that your whole creation
may find fulfilment in the Son of Man,
Jesus Christ our Saviour. Amen.

65   May the richness of your creation, Lord,
and the mystery of your providence
lead us to that heavenly city
where all peoples will bring their wealth,
forsake their sins and find their true joy,
Jesus Christ our Lord. Amen.

96   Lord God, you draw us by your beauty
and transform us by your holiness;
let our worship echo all creation's praise
and declare your glory to the nations;
through Jesus Christ our Lord. Amen.

98   Lord God, just and true,
you make your salvation known in the sight of the nations;
tune the song of our hearts to the music of creation
as you come among us to judge the earth;
through our Saviour Jesus Christ. Amen.

126 Lord, as you send rain and flowers
even to the wilderness,
renew us by your Holy Spirit,
help us to sow good seed in time of adversity
and to live to rejoice in your good harvest of all creation;
through Jesus Christ our Lord. Amen.

Readings on Creation and the Environment

Old Testament Readings

A cosmic hymn of praise	Genesis 1.1–2.3
The garden of creation	Genesis 24b–19
Creation restored after the deluge	Genesis 8.12–22
God's promise to sustain creation	Genesis 9.8–17
God's provision	Exodus 16.11–15
A feast of fruitfulness	Leviticus 23.33–43
The promise of a fertile land	Leviticus 26.1–13
God's gifts to the redeemed	Deuteronomy 6.9–14
The gift of the land	Deuteronomy 8.7–18
Offering of the first-fruits	Deuteronomy 26.1–11
The promise of restoration	Amos 9.13
The covenant of peace with all creation	Hosea 2.18–23
Repentance and restoration	Hosea 14.2–10
The harmony of animal kingdom in the messianic age	Isaiah 11.1–9a
Feasting in God's presence	Isaiah 25.6–9; 55.6–11
The blossoming of the wilderness at God's appearing	Isaiah 35.1–7
The whole cosmic scope of praise for God's redemption	Isaiah 55.12–end
A sign of a fruitful future	Jeremiah 32.6–15
God promises his people a peaceable land	Ezekiel 34.25–31
The hope of humankind restored	Ezekiel 37.1–14
A vision of waters restoring the land	Ezekiel 47.[1–6a] 6b–12
The wonder of creation	Ecclesiasticus 42.15—43.12
A garden as symbol of divine love	Song of Songs 4.12–13
Kinship and the land	Ruth 2.1–13
Defiant nature and the hope of immortality	Job 14.7–10
The rich minerals of the earth	Job 28.1–6
God's majesty and creation's marvel	Job 38.1–11, 16–18
God's wisdom and creation	Proverbs 8.1–4, 22–31

Readings from the Apocrypha

The wonders of creation	Ecclesiasticus 42.15–33
Blessing of the forest	Judith 16.13–15
The praises of creation	Song of the Three, vv.28–59;
	Jubilees 2.21–27

New Testament Readings

The natural world longing for liberation	Romans 8.18–22
The risen Christ appears in the garden, prefiguring a new creation	John 20.15
Christ as the new creation	Colossians 1.1–15
Creation renewed for the healing of the nations	Revelation 22.1–5
God's generosity and human gratitude	2 Corinthians 9.9–11a
Sufficiency of resources and simplicity of lifestyle	1 Timothy 6.7–10, 17–19; or Matthew 6.25–34
The risen Christ and the abundance of life	John 21.1–14
The promise of paradise restored	Revelation 2.1–7

Gospel Readings

The book of nature	Matthew 6.25–34
The Lord of nature brings peace to violent discord	Mark 4.35–41
Nurturing the fig tree	Luke 13.6–9
From the seed to a tree of life: an image of God's reign	Mark 4.30–32 (or Luke 13.18–19; Matthew 13.31–32)
Hungry people fed on Christ's abundance	John 6.1–13
God's people as a fruitful vine	John 15.1–17

The Feast of the Holy Cross (14 September)[10]

Festival – Red

The cross on which our Lord was crucified has become the universal symbol for Christianity. After the end of the persecution era, early in the fourth century, pilgrims began to travel to Jerusalem to visit and pray at the places associated with the life of Jesus. Helena, the mother of the emperor, was a Christian and, whilst overseeing excavations in the city, is said to have uncovered a cross, which many believed to be the Cross of Christ. A basilica was built on the site of the Holy Sepulchre and dedicated on this day in the year 335.

On this feast day, set as it is in September and potentially therefore in the middle of a creation season, there is an opportunity to reflect on the cosmic significance of the cross. In Christian liturgy, the cross is often represented as the tree of life, a sign of the new life that comes to us through Christ's death and resurrection. In preparing the disciples for the fate that awaited him, Jesus spoke of his impending suffering and death on the cross as being like a grain of wheat that falls into the earth and dies: 'if it dies, it bears much fruit.' (John 12.24).

Collect

Almighty God,
who in the passion of your blessed Son
made an instrument of painful death
to be for us the means of life and peace:
grant us so to glory in the cross of Christ
that we may gladly suffer for his sake;
who is alive and reigns with you,
in the unity of the Holy Spirit,
one God, now and for ever.

All Amen.

Readings

Old Testament	Numbers 21.4–9
Psalm	22.23–28
New Testament	Philippians 2.6–11
Gospel	John 3.13–17

---

[10] For full liturgical provision, see Common Worship: Festivals pp.102–107

Post Communion

> Faithful God,
> whose Son bore our sins in his body on the tree
> and gave us this sacrament to show forth his death until he comes:
> give us grace to glory in the cross of our Lord Jesus Christ,
> for he is our salvation, our life and our hope,
> who reigns as Lord, now and for ever.

All Amen.

Short Reflections

Hymns on the Cross by Venantius Fortunatus

> O Faithful Cross, amongst all trees the only noble Tree,
> No other wood has grown a tree of such leaves, flowers, and fruit.
> O sweet wood, sweet nails, how sweet the burden that you bear.
>
> *Crux Fidelis*

> O sweet and noble wood,
> on your boughs you bear fruit so rare.
> You are planted where the water flows,
> and your spreading branches are adorned with flowers.
> On your branches hangs the vine
> from which blood-red sweet wine flows.
>
> *Crux Benedicta*

'In Adoration of the Cross' by Saint Theodore of Studios

> How precious is the gift of the cross, how splendid to
> contemplate! In the cross, there is no mingling of good and
> evil, as in the tree of paradise: it is wholly beautiful to behold
> and good to taste. The fruit of this tree is not death but life,
> not darkness but light. This tree does not cast us out of
> paradise, but opens the way for our return. This was the tree
> on which Christ, like a king on a chariot, destroyed the devil,
> the lord of death, and freed the human race from tyranny.
> This was the tree upon which the Lord, like a brave warrior
> wounded in hands, feet and side, healed the wounds of sin
> that the evil serpent had inflicted on our nature. A tree once
> caused our death, but now a tree brings us life.

A Meditation on the Holy Cross by Saint Anselm

Holy Cross, recalling the cross of our Lord Jesus Christ,
that brings us back from the abyss of eternal death
and leads us to the eternal life we had lost by sin.

I glory in that cross, and by the cross I adore our merciful Lord
and what in mercy he has done for us.

The cross by which we are sealed for God,
glorious cross, we ought to glory only in you.
By you the world is renewed and made beautiful with truth.

Abridged

Propers for St Francis (4 October)

Lesser Festival – Religious – White

Collect

> O God, you ever delight to reveal yourself
> to the childlike and lowly of heart:
> grant that, following the example of the blessed Francis,
> we may count the wisdom of this world as foolishness
> and know only Jesus Christ and him crucified,
> who is alive and reigns with you,
> in the unity of the Holy Spirit,
> one God, now and for ever.

All **Amen.**

Old Testament   Micah 6.6–8

Responsorial Psalm

> **R   Be joyful in the Lord, all the earth:**
> **[give thanks and bless his name].**

O be joyful in the Lord, all the earth;
serve the Lord with gladness
and come before his presence with a song. **R**

Know that Lord is God;
it is he that has made us and we are his;
we are his people and the sheep of his pasture. **R**

Enter his gates with thanksgiving
and his courts with praise;
give thanks to him and bless his name. **R**

For the Lord is gracious;
his steadfast love is everlasting,
and his faithfulness endures from generation to generation. **R**

Psalm 100

New Testament	Galatians 6.14–18
Gospel	Luke 12.22–34

Post Communion

Lord God,
you made your church rich
through the poverty of blessed Francis:
help us like him to sing creation's praise,
and care for all your creatures;
through Jesus Christ, our crucified and risen Lord.

All **Amen.**

APPENDIX – OTHER SOURCES OF MATERIAL

Church of England website Creationtide Resources (includes discussion materials and other suggestions)
https://www.churchofengland.org/more/policy-and-thinking/our-views/environment-and-climate-change/creationtide/creationtide

Church Support Hub: https://churchsupporthub.org/?s=Harvest

Celebrating Festivals Together: https://spckpublishing.co.uk/festivals-together

Creative Ideas for Wild Church: Taking all-age worship and learning outdoors Mary Jackson & Juno Hollyhock, Canterbury Press 2016: https://chbookshop.hymnsam.co.uk/books/9781848258815/creative-ideas-for-wild-church

God's Good Earth: Praise and Prayer for Creation by Anne & Jeffery Rowthorn, Liturgical Press 2018: https://chbookshop.hymnsam.co.uk/books/9780814644126/gods-good-earth

Together for a Season: All-age resources for Feasts and Festivals of the Christian Year Ed. Gill Ambrose, CHP 2009: www.chpublishing.co.uk/books/9780715140642/together-for-a-season-feasts-and-festivals

WorshipWorkshop (schools worship resources, website originally created by the Liturgical Commission and colleagues from the National Society, now completely independent of the Liturgical Commission): https://www.worshipworkshop.org.uk/search/?searchTerm=Harvest

The website of the *Anglican Communion Environmental Network* (ACEN) gives links to documents and resources from a number of areas of the Anglican Communion. See http://acen.anglicancommunion.org/resources.documents.cfm

The *Anglican Church of Southern Africa* has provided a substantial collection of study and reference material and resources for worship. This can be found on the ACEN website at: http://www.anglicancommunion.org/resources/docs/season–of–creation.pdf

The *Anglican Church of Australia* also has a fine collection of liturgical material on the ACEN website.

The *Episcopal Ecological Network* (TEC) offers online resources for the Season of Creation, normally observed during the Season of Pentecost. This has not been updated since 2011. See http://econline.org/reflect/liturgy/com

CTBI has resources entitled *'Time for Creation'* (1 September–4 October). See www.ctbi.org.uk

The *European Christian Environmental Network* provides material at: http://ecen.org/cms/index.php?page=creationtime

The Report by ChurchCare (The Cathedrals and Church Buildings Division), entitled *Shrinking the Footprint*, includes worship and study resources: http://www.churchcare.co.uk/shrinking–the–footprint

Alliance of Religions and Conservation – resources: http://www.arcworld.org/news.asp?pageID=408

Sharing Eden – a book setting out interfaith responses to environmental and creation–related issues: http://www.sharingeden.org/

Operation Noah provides a good variety of material for worship. Though this is not authorised by the Church of England, it comes recommended by Diocesan Environmental Officers: http://www.operationnoah.org/sites/default/files/Liturgy_materials_0.pdf

Bishop David Hamid (Diocese of Europe) blogged about planning for the Season of Creation during 2011: http://eurobishop.blogspot.co.uk/2011/08/creationtide–liturgy–planning.html

Dr Jeremy Clines, Chaplain of Sheffield University, has published his PhD thesis, Earthing Common Worship: an ecotheological critique of the Common Worship texts of the Church of England (Birmingham, 2011) at http://etheses.bham.ac.uk/2838/